A Study in the Book of Daniel
The Kingdom of Heaven in Prophecy

I0460082

M J Tiry

A Study in the Book of Daniel
The Kingdom of Heaven in Prophecy

Daniel 2:44 (KJV) And in the days of these kings shall the God of heaven set up a kingdom, which shall never be destroyed: and the kingdom shall not be left to other people, *but* it shall break in pieces and consume all these kingdoms, and it shall stand for ever.

M J Tiry

M J Tiry

A Study in the Book of Daniel
The Kingdom of Heaven in Prophecy

A Study in the Book of Daniel -- The Kingdom of Heaven in Prophecy / M J Tiry

ISBN

Paper Back:	979-8-9918240-2-6
Hard Cover	979-8-9918240-1-9
eBook	979-8-9918240-2-6

Library of Congress Control Number 2025901593

Printed in the United States of America

Published April 6 2025

Published by M J Tiry Publishing
hippewa Falls, WI 54729

DEDICATION

This Study is dedicated to you the student of the Word of God. May this be edifying and encouraging to you as you engage yourself in the quest for Bible truth.

CONTENTS

Table of Contents

Tables:

Abbreviations used:

c.	circa ("about/Approximately")
cp	Compare
e.g.	exampligratia ("for example")
et. al.	Et allii ("and others")
etc.	Et. cetara ("and so forth")
ff	and the following (verses, pages, etc.)
i.e.	id. est. (that is)
vs, vv	verse (s)
viz.	Videlicet ('namely")

Refernces Cited:

The Coming Prince – Sir Robert Anderson / 1894

Daniel in the Critic's Den – Sir Robert Anderson / 1909

The CI Schofield Reference Bible – Oxford University Press 1909

Notes to the Reader:

A word is in order here on how to study the Bible and actually how to approach the Bible. Some basic principles to hold in our study of Scripture then are:

1. All of scripture came from the mouth of God and it fully equips the man of God to do anything that God would have him do. "All scripture *is* given by inspiration of God, and *is* profitable for doctrine, for reproof, for correction, for instruction in righteousness: That the man of God may be perfect, throughly furnished unto all good works." (2Timothy 3:16-17) It can be said that the Holy Spirit never works apart from the Bible and the Bible never works apart from the Holy Spirit.

2. The term "inspiration of God" in 2Timothy 3:16 means that it was breathed out of God's mouth. It is truly as the Lord tells the devil in Matthew 4:4 "It is written; Man shall not live by bread alone, but by every word that proceedeth out of the mouth of God." And that is the origin of every word of scripture – from the mouth of God.

3. Scripture must be studied in its context in order for it to make sense. There are two contexts: the immediate context in which the passage is set and there is the remote context that looks at the Bible as a whole. Billy Sunday is said to have made the statement "A text without a context is a pretext." That concept is what Peter is communicating when he said in 2Peter 1:20 & 21 "Knowing this first, that no prophecy of the scripture is of any private interpretation. For the prophecy came not in old time by the will of man: but holy men of God spake *as they were* moved by the Holy Ghost." No passage of scripture is intended to stand by itself but rather each passage actually relates to every other passage of scripture. One of the greatest tools to Bible study is a good cross reference (one that I like is The Treasury of Scripture Knowledge). By comparing scripture with scripture the Bible teaches itself. The Bible itself is its greatest and best teacher.

4. While all of scripture is written for our learning, not every passage of scripture is addressed to us. The word of truth then must be rightly divided. Paul tells us this in 2Timothy 2:15 saying "Study to shew thyself approved unto God, a workman that needeth not to be ashamed, rightly dividing the word of truth." We trust that Appendix 4 of this book will be very helpful in seeing this concept.

5. Another key to understanding the Bible is simply to let it say what it clearly says. It is a major mistake to spiritualize scripture. The Bible is written to be taken literally. There are times when the Bible uses figures of speech (figurative language) and when it does it is apparent that is the case. Basically, we must remember the adage "if the literal sense makes perfect sense, seek no other sense."

6. God has taken great care to give us His inspired word and gave it without error. He has also pledged to preserve it so. (Psalm 12:6-7) "The words of the LORD *are* pure words: *as* silver tried in a furnace of earth, purified seven times. Thou shalt keep them, O LORD, thou shalt preserve them from this generation for ever." It is the conviction of this author that there exists today a preserved text of the inspired and inerrant Word of God. This is not in the originals for they have been lost through time but this preservation of scripture is in the multiplicity of copies. It was God's desire and design that the Bible gets into the hands of the people. If there is a doctrine of preservation, then that preservation is done in the multiplicity of copies. This author holds the conviction that the preserved text line is the Received Text (Majority Text) of the New Testament and the Masoretic Text of the Hebrew Old Testament. Since there is only one translation in print in English today from these, all scripture references in this study are from the King James Bible.

7. There is yet another key to an effective study of the word of God. That is the heart attitude of the Bereans of Acts 17:11. They received the Word with an open mind but they did not just take any man's word for truth or error of what was said until they searched it out in the scripture. That approach gave them protection from error for they made the Word of God their final authority and examined what everyone said based on the Word of Truth – the Bible.

8. One final thing regarding the Bible having the impact in our lives that God intended is the simple matter of believing it. Paul tells the Thessalonians that they received the word of God, they received it not as the word of men but as it is in truth the word of God, which "...effectually worketh in you that believe." It is not just

the understanding of it that makes it effective but applying it by faith to one's life that makes it effective to give spiritual strength and vitality.

9. The author has a series of four books in what is called the Prophecy Series. This book is the first in the series. The second of this series is *"Matthew's Gospel- Study of the King and His Kingdom."* The third in the series is *"A Study in Hebrews – Israel and the New Covenant."*. The fourth and last in the series is *"A Study in the Revelation—the End Times Fulfillment of Bible Prophecy."*

PREFACE

The Bible is laid out in clearly defined sections that show the dispensations as they unfold in time. The two-fold purpose of God is presented in a sequence that was determined by God and sequentially revealed to man. The revelation of the Word of God was revealed as it was needed for man to respond in faith to what God was telling him to do. There are two programs whereby God interacts with man. The majority of the Bible is involved with the program that is called Bible Prophecy. That program centers in the nation of Israel and concerns a kingdom that God will one day set up on earth under the reign of the promised Messiah. That kingdom is called the Kingdom of Heaven in Matthew's gospel. The other program is called "the Mystery" and involves a body of believers called "the church, which is His Body." The program called "the Mystery" is revealed in the Bible in the Pauline epistles and is referred to as "The Dispensation of the Grace of God."

To understand the Bible, it is helpful to see that the two programs are revealed in the five sections of the Bible as shown bellow. The Old Testament presents the promise of the Kingdom of Heaven in prophecy. The four gospels (and particularly Matthew's gospel) present the Kingdom of Heaven as being "at Hand" – it was ready to be set up. The Book of Acts presents the offer of the Kingdom of Heaven to Israel and Israel's rejection of the offer when the nation rejected the resurrected King and thus also the Kingdom. The Book of Acts also reveals the sending of Paul to the world as the apostle of the Gentiles. The Pauline epistles then present the Dispensation of Grace as a temporary postponement of the establishment of the Kingdom of Heaven. Finally, the books of Hebrews through Revelation present the establishment of the Kingdom on earth. There are four key books in the Bible that deal with the kingdom established on earth -- those being Daniel which sees the kingdom in prophecy, Matthew which sees the kingdom of heaven as being at hand, Hebrews which presents Jesus Christ as the High Priest of Israel who will return as Israel's redeemer, and the Revelation which finally presents the establishment of the kingdom.

The Book of Daniel presents the Lord Jesus Christ as the rightful king who will reign over Israel and the earth in the kingdom. It is called "The Kingdom of Heaven" in Matthew's gospel because when it is set up, God's will is going to be done in the earth as it is in heaven (Matt. 6:10)when that Kingdom is set up.

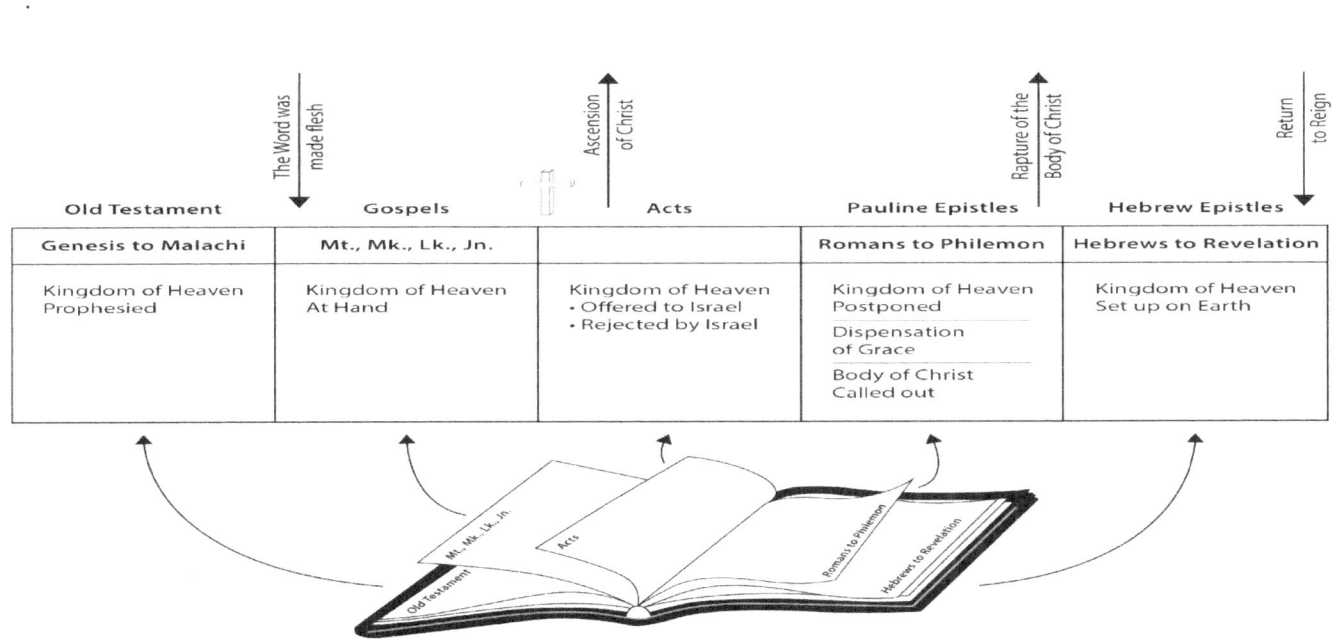

Old Testament	Gospels	Acts	Pauline Epistles	Hebrew Epistles
Genesis to Malachi	Mt., Mk., Lk., Jn.		Romans to Philemon	Hebrews to Revelation
Kingdom of Heaven Prophesied	Kingdom of Heaven At Hand	Kingdom of Heaven • Offered to Israel • Rejected by Israel	Kingdom of Heaven Postponed / Dispensation of Grace / Body of Christ Called out	Kingdom of Heaven Set up on Earth

The Progression of Revelation to Man

ACKNOWLEDGMENTS

I thank the Lord Jesus Christ for redeeming my soul and the souls of believers through the ages by His sacrifice of His perfect life at Calvary. I thank God also for the regenerating work of the Holy Spirit of God for quickening my spirit that I might understand the Word of God. I thank our heavenly Father for all He is and for the riches of His grace in which He has made us believers accepted in His beloved Son. I thank Him for the very Word of God that he has given to us and that we can study it in our own language. I appreciate the students of the Word with whom I share a great passion for study of the Bible to learn of the eternal blessings that are there for our learning and edification. I particularly appreciate the series of messages presented by Richard Jordan of the Grace School of the Bible for the insight that his diligent teaching on the book of Matthew has provided.

I thank my daughters for their help in putting this work together and for the publishing process. I would not be able to do it without their help. I thank Vince Kison and David Swanson for their work in review of this book.

Introduction

The Book of Daniel is a key book in understanding Bible prophecy. Prophecy centers in the nation of Israel and the role that the nation will play in God's plan for the earth. God's purpose for Israel is stated in the covenant that God made with Abraham in Genesis 22:17-18 "¹⁷That in blessing I will bless thee, and in multiplying I will multiply thy seed as the stars of the heaven, and as the sand which *is* upon the sea shore; and thy seed shall possess the gate of his enemies; ¹⁸And in thy seed shall all the nations of the earth be blessed; because thou hast obeyed my voice."

The key verse in the book of Daniel is in Chapter 2 Verse 44 "⁴⁴And in the days of these kings shall the God of heaven set up a kingdom, which shall never be destroyed: and the kingdom shall not be left to other people, *but* it shall break in pieces and consume all these kingdoms, and it shall stand for ever." One day God will establish a kingdom on the earth through the nation of Israel. It is called in scripture "the Kingdom of Heaven" because the God of heaven will set it up. However, at the writing of the book of Daniel, the nation is being taken into captivity for its sin and rebellion to God. God's purpose in the book of Daniel is to communicate to Israel and to the nations that He is using Israel's captivity to bring in the "Times of the Gentiles" (i.e. the rule of the Gentiles over Israel and the world) but only as a temporary situation. He is doing it for the chastening of the disobedient nation.

The term "…the times of the Gentiles…" (Luke 21:24) is not to be confused with the term "…the fullness of the Gentiles…" as Paul uses the term in Romans 11:25. The "fullness of the Gentiles" is a reference to the completion (the closing) of the present dispensation of grace. During this present dispensation, God is calling out the church which is Christ's Body – a Gentile church. The church of the present dispensation of grace in nowhere to be found in the Book of Daniel because the church which is Christ's Body is the subject of the mystery that was kept secret until the Lord revealed it to and through Paul (the apostle of the Gentiles – Romans 11:13; 16:25; and Ephesians 3:1-3). The times of the Gentiles began when Israel was taken captive and lost her sovereignty as a nation. The Book of Daniel then lays out the Gentile political future from the time of the captivity of Israel under Nebuchnezzar through time to the kingdom of the antichrist and ultimately to the establishment of the Kingdom of Heaven.

The general theme of the book is found in Daniel 4:17 "¹⁷This matter *is* by the decree of the watchers, and the demand by the word of the holy ones: to the intent that the living may know that the most High ruleth in the kingdom of men, and giveth it to whomsoever he will, and setteth up over it the basest of men." (See also verses 25 & 32 of the same chapter). God's purpose is to establish the Kingdom of Heaven when God's will (His determined purpose) is going to "…be done in earth as it is in heaven" (Matt. 6:10). Until that time, the prophecy of the Book of Daniel will govern the affairs of men except for the fact that the entire program was interrupted by the mystery revealed through Paul. We will see more of that when we study chapter nine of the book.

The Book of Daniel has been criticized by liberal theologians who claim it is a forgery. However, the book is quoted or referenced in other scripture written about the same time. (E.g. Ezekiel 14:14, 20 and 28:3). The Lord Himself referred to Daniel and his prophecies in Matthew 24:15. The writer of Hebrews probably had Daniel in view in Hebrews 11:33 with the reference to stopping of the mouth of lions. The fulfillment of Bible prophecy is what separated the Bible from other books. Prophecy is "…a light that shineth in a dark place, until the day dawn, and the day star arise in your hearts" (2Peter 1:19). In prophecy, "…holy men of God [such as Daniel] spoke as they were moved by the Holy Ghost…" (2Peter 1:21).

Some of the historical background to the book is helpful to set the stage to the historical portion of the book. Josiah was the last godly king of Judah before the Babylonian captivity. Josiah died at Megiddo in a battle with the king of Assyria (2Kings 23:29). Jehoahaz his son became king in his place. Jehoahaz was a wicked king and was removed by Pharaohnechoh who then made Eliakim (also know as Jehoiakim, Jehoahaz' brother) king. Nebuchadnezzar, the king of Babylon came to besiege Jerusalem about 606 BC during the reign (three years into the reign) of Jehoiakim. Jerusalem was taken in about 604 BC and the first captives were taken in this siege. Daniel and his three friends were among them. The city was not destroyed at this siege. At Jehoiakim's death, his son Jehoiachin replaced him as king. Jehoiachin rebelled against Nebuchadnezzar and the city was again besieged in 598 BC. Again more captives were taken and more of the vessels of the house of the Lord were taken, but again the city was not destroyed. It is probable that the prophet Ezekiel was taken captive in this deportation (2Kings 24:6-16). Zedekiah (an uncle to Jehoiachin) was made king. He also rebelled against Nebuchadnezzar, only to have the city destroyed and the temple burned and have his sons slain in his presence. A third and final deportation went into captivity in about 588 BC. All of this was done in fulfillment of Jeremiah 25:8-13; 2Kings 20:18-19; and Isaiah 39:7.

Jeremiah 25:8-14 (KJV) [8] Therefore thus saith the LORD of hosts; Because ye have not heard my words, [9] Behold, I will send and take all the families of the north, saith the LORD, and Nebuchadrezzar the king of Babylon, my servant, and will bring them against this land, and against the inhabitants thereof, and against all these nations round about, and will utterly destroy them, and make them an astonishment, and an hissing, and perpetual desolations. [10] Moreover I will take from them the voice of mirth, and the voice of gladness, the voice of the bridegroom, and the voice of the bride, the sound of the millstones, and the light of the candle. [11] And this whole land shall be a desolation, *and* an astonishment; and these nations shall serve the king of Babylon seventy years. [12] And it shall come to pass, when seventy years are accomplished, *that* I will punish the king of Babylon, and that nation, saith the LORD, for their iniquity, and the land of the Chaldeans, and will make it perpetual desolations. [13] And I will bring upon that land all my words which I have pronounced against it, *even* all that is written in this book, which Jeremiah hath prophesied against all the nations. [14] For many nations and great kings shall serve themselves of them also: and I will recompense them according to their deeds, and according to the works of their own hands.

The Law and Israel's Captivity -- Five Courses of Judgment

To understand the book of Daniel, we need to first understand why God had Israel lose its sovereignty and go into captivity. Israel was a covenant people. God had made a series of covenants with the nation starting with the covenant that He made with Abraham in Genesis Chapter 22. However, the covenant that comes into play regarding the captivity of the nation is the Mosaic Covenant. This is what is called the Law Covenant or the Covenant of the Law. The Law Covenant was actually a legally binding agreement between God and the nation. It was a system of blessing and cursing as we see in Deuteronomy 11:26-28.

"²⁶ Behold, I set before you this day a blessing and a curse; ²⁷ A blessing, if ye obey the commandments of the LORD your God, which I command you this day: ²⁸ And a curse, if ye will not obey the commandments of the LORD your God, but turn aside out of the way which I command you this day, to go after other gods, which ye have not known.". (Deuteronomy 11:26-28)

The Mosaic Covenant was a conditional covenant. One of the more salient points of the Law is found in Leviticus Chapter 26 where we find that there will be five successive courses of judgment that would come upon Israel for their failure to keep the Law. The table below (Table 2) lays out those successive courses. Because Israel agreed to the covenant of the Law, they were bound by the terms of the Law. It was legally binding contract with a system of blessings and curses.

The captivity of the nation was the last of the five successive courses of judgment. During each of these courses, God sent a prophet to the nation to call Israel back from the apostasy that had gripped the nation and brought them to that judgment which was needed to recover the nation. The Old Testament is the history of these successive courses of judgment on the nation. In fact, the successive courses of judgment become the framework for the Old Testament Scriptures from Judges through Malachi. The nation would go into declension only to recover under the rule of the judge or the prophet that brought them through it only to go into the next course of declension and judgment.

These five courses of judgment are a sad commentary on the spiritual life of Israel under the Law. It is a story of the people that God set aside from the rest of the Gentile nations as His people failing under the Law covenant. The first course of judgment was under the rule of the judges. When the nation went into apostasy it was judged by adversity from her enemies. With each round of adversity, God raised up a judge to bring deliverance to the nation. The second course came in the reign of Rehoboam (Solomon's son). We notice that between the first and the second course, there is a bright spot in Israel's history – that of the reign of David and his son Solomon. This bright spot gave Israel a glimpse of the coming future reign of Jesus Christ who will sit on David's throne in the promised Kingdom.

As we study this key book of Bible prophecy, we will be seeing the times of the Gentiles laid out as a series of Gentile kingdoms that rise successively to prominence only to be replaced with another Gentile kingdom. What we see in this book of prophecy is the line of the Gentiles kingdoms that comprise the Times of the Gentiles from the captivity by Babylon to reign of the antichrist. What we do not see is the information concerning the present dispensation of grace because that was still a mystery that was hid in God.

Table 1 Five Successive Courses of Judgment

Verse	Course of Judgment		Main Prophet	Books
Lev 26:14-17	1. Physical illnesses and afflictions Enemy raids and defeat in battle Tributary rival by border enemies.		Samuel	Judges
	Davidic Interlude			I Sam 16 – I Kings 12
Lev 26:18-20	2. Internal government problems; cursing of the Land and its environment.		Elijah	I Kings 12 to 22
Lev 26:21-22	3. Increase severity of land judgments affliction from wild beasts.		Elisha	II Kings 1 to 10:31
Lev 26:23-26	4. Greater oppression by enemies Occupation of the land Lengthy and persistent sieges.		Isaiah	II Kings 10:32 to 16:20
Lev 26:27ff	5. National destruction and captivity. Removal from the land Captivity of the nation.	Babylon Persia Greece Rome Antichrist	Jeremiah Daniel Malachi John the Baptist The Apostle John	2 Kings 17:1-25:30 Ezra, Nehemiah, Esther *Silence Matthew to Acts Hebrews to Revelation

* From Malachi to Mathew, God was silent. He would be giving no communication to indicate to them that they were His people. Therefore, at the conclusion of the fourth curse and the beginning of the fifth curse, God had many of His Prophets write down the prophecies of the coming judgment, the reason for the judgment and the glory that would follow with the reign of the Messiah.

The Law and Israel's Future

Because of Israel's failure under the Law, and because the nation was under a binding covenant with the Mosaic Law, Israel was bound to live with the consequences of the broken law. However, it is God's intention that Israel will have the land that He promised to Israel through Abraham. Therefore, He makes another covenant with Israel that he lays "beside the covenant that He made with them in Horeb." (Deuteronomy 29:1) This is what we call the Palestinian Covenant. This Covenant is spelled out in Deuteronomy 30:1-10. The Law was supplemented by the Palestinians Covenant so that Israel will one day have the Promised Land in spite of the fact that they failed under the Law of Moses. They disqualified themselves from possessing the land. Basically, the covenant says to Israel: "Yes you failed to keep the law, and yes, you will bear the consequences by being taken out of the land but I will bring you back into the land after you have been expelled."

The Mosaic Covenant and Us

The Law was taken out of the way for us who live in the dispensation of grace. (Colossians 2:14). Our relationship to God is not now nor has it ever been on the basis of Law. We are free from the Law (Galatians 5:1) that we might serve as sons in God's family. Grace consistently applied by faith will produce in us that obedience which the Law demanded but could not produce (Romans 8:4).

The Palestinian Covenant

The Covenant that we call the Palestinian Covenant is found in Deuteronomy 28:63 through 30:10. It is so called because it gives the conditions under which Israel will enter the Promised Land in spite of the fact that they disqualified themselves from re-entering by their failure under the Mosaic Covenant. Israel has never yet possessed all of the land that was promised them in Genesis 15:18 and Numbers 34:1-12. God through Moses made the Palestinian Covenant some 40 years after the Mosaic Covenant (the Law) was made. The Law was conditional with potential for both blessing and cursing.

The Bible Prophecy Series

This study *"A Study in the Book of Daniel – the Kingdom of Heaven in Prophecy."* in Daniel is the first book in the author's "Prophecy Series." Bible prophecy consists of essentially the entire Bible outside of the Pauline Epistles. The author has a series of four books in what is called the Prophecy Series. The second of this series is *"Matthew's Gospel- Study of the King and His Kingdom."* The third in the series is *"A Study in Hebrews – Israel and the New Covenant."* The fourth and last in the series is *"A Study in the Revelation—the End Times Fulfillment of Bible Prophecy."* The Pauline Epistles comprise the realm of Bible doctrine called "the preaching of Jesus Christ according to the revelation of the mystery." While prophecy concerns a kingdom that will be set up on earth under the reign of Jesus Christ as Israel's Messiah, the mystery concerns the Lord Jesus Christ as the head of the church which is Christ's body – a Gentile church. For the Bible student who desires to go deeper into a study of the mystery, the book *"More than Conquerors – a Study in the Book of Romans,"* and the book *"You and Your Creator – A Study in God's Eternal Purpose for Man"* by this same author will provide in depth study in how we who live in the present dispensation of the grace of God are to live as members of the church, which is His body.

Introduction: Study Guide Questions

1. What is the key verse of Daniel?

2. What is the difference between "the times of the Gentiles" and "the fullness of the Gentiles?"

3. What verse in Daniel states the general theme of the book?

4. List one Old Testament and two New Testament passages that quote or allude to Daniel that prove Daniel is not a forgery.

5. Who was the last godly king of Israel?

Chapter 1
Captivity and Personal History of Daniel

Daniel 1:1-2

"¹ In the third year of the reign of Jehoiakim king of Judah came Nebuchadnezzar king of Babylon unto Jerusalem, and besieged it. ² And the Lord gave Jehoiakim king of Judah into his hand, with part of the vessels of the house of God: which he carried into the land of Shinar to the house of his god; and he brought the vessels into the treasure house of his god." (Dan 1:1 & 2)

Captivity of the last Three Kings of Israel

In Ezekiel 21:25-27, God prophesies through Ezekiel that the crown will fall from Israel until Messiah comes. We know that this will happen not at His birth and His first earthy ministry but at His second advent.

Ezekiel 21:24-27 ²⁴ Therefore thus saith the Lord GOD; Because ye have made your iniquity to be remembered, in that your transgressions are discovered, so that in all your doings your sins do appear; because, *I say*, that ye are come to remembrance, ye shall be taken with the hand. ²⁵ And thou, profane wicked prince of Israel, whose day is come, when iniquity *shall have* an end, ²⁶ Thus saith the Lord GOD; Remove the diadem, and take off the crown: this *shall* not *be* the same: exalt *him that is* low, and abase *him that is* high. ²⁷ I will overturn, overturn, overturn, it: and it shall be no *more*, until he come whose right it is; and I will give it *him*.

In Ezekiel 36:16-24, God gives the reason for the captivity. God brought the judgment of the captivity for the sake of His holy name, for the defiling that the nation did while in the land.

Ezekiel 36:16-24 ¹⁶ Moreover the word of the LORD came unto me, saying, ¹⁷ Son of man, when the house of Israel dwelt in their own land, they defiled it by their own way and by their doings: their way was before me as the uncleanness of a removed woman. ¹⁸ Wherefore I poured my fury upon them for the blood that they had shed upon the land, and for their idols *wherewith* they had polluted it: ¹⁹ And I scattered them among the heathen, and they were dispersed through the countries: according to their way and according to their doings I judged them. ²⁰ And when they entered unto the heathen, whither they went, they profaned my holy name, when they said to them, These *are* the people of the LORD, and are gone forth out of his land. ²¹ But I had pity for mine holy name, which the house of Israel had profaned among the heathen, whither they went. ²² Therefore say unto the house of Israel, Thus saith the Lord GOD; I do not *this* for your sakes, O house of Israel, but for mine holy name's sake, which ye have profaned among the heathen, whither ye went. ²³ And I will sanctify my great name, which was profaned among the heathen, which ye have profaned in the midst of them; and the heathen shall know that I *am* the LORD, saith the Lord GOD, when I shall be sanctified in you before their eyes. ²⁴ For I will take you from among the heathen, and gather you out of all countries, and will bring you into your own land.

There is a three step process in the failure of Israel politically as represented by the three step captivity.

- First we see the captivity of Jehoiakim (2Chron. 36:5-7).
- Then came the captivity of Jehoiachin (2Chron. 36:8-9)
- Finally the captivity of Zedekiah (2Chronicals 36:11-13) who was then blinded (2Kings 25:6).

Three steps in Israel's Failure in the New Testament

- In the New Testament Scriptures, we see a three step failure of Israel spiritually.
- John the Baptist was sent to Israel by the Father with the message "repent for the Kingdom of Heaven is at hand." But this message was rejected (Matt. 21:25-27).
- The Lord Jesus Christ comes to Israel with the same message but His message too was rejected as we see in Matthew 12:22-32 in the response of the Pharisees when He cast out the devil that made the man blind and dumb. In this passage in Matthew 12 we see the Lord introducing the unforgivable sin. They were blaspheming the Son by alleging that the works that the Son was doing was done by power Beelzebub the prince of devils (verse 24). The Lord defined that as blasphemy against the Son. He then announces to the Pharisees and the nation at large that they could be forgiven for blasphemy against the Son but to do so against the Holy Ghost will not be forgiven (verses 31-32).
- The Holy Ghost proclaims the message through the twelve and men like Stephen (Stephen is the messenger of Luke 19:12-14) that Jesus Christ, the one who the nation had crucified, is Israel's Messiah and that He was raised from the dead to sit on the throne of David. However, that message from the Holy Ghost also was rejected. Finally, in Acts 13:6, a blind Barjesus (whose name means "son of Jehovah Savior") becomes a representation in type of Israel as a nation – a nation that is blinded in part until the fullness of the Gentiles is come in (Romans 11:7, 11, 25).

A Three Step Process in the Glory of God leaving the Temple

There is an interesting three step withdrawal of the Glory of God in Ezekiel that corresponds to the three step departure of God from Israel in the Book of Acts.

In Ezekiel we see:

- In Ezekiel 9:3 and 10:4 the Glory moves from the Cherub to the threshold.
- In Ezekiel 10:18-22 from the threshold it leaves the temple to go to the Mount of Olives.
- In Ezekiel 11:23 it leaves the Mount of Olives, from thence it departs.

Three steps in the Lord's departure from the Temple in Matthew's Gospel

The Lord left the temple in much the same way.

- In Mathew 23:38, he leaves and pronounces that "your house is left to you desolate." Earlier, He referred to the Temple as "My Father's house" (Matthew 21:13).
- In Mathew 24:2 he announces its destruction saying that "there shall not be left one stone of the temple left upon another."
- From there he goes to the Mount of Olives and gives the famous Olivet discourse in the rest of Chapter 24 of Matthew. Later He ascended to heaven from that Mount of Olives (Acts 1:9, 12). One day He will return to that same spot (Zech. 14:4).

Three is a three step process in God turning to the Gentiles in the book of Acts

In Acts we see a three step announcement in God turning to the Gentiles with the gospel of the grace of God.

- In Acts 13: 44-46   Paul says "we turn to the Gentiles."
- In Acts 18:6   Paul says "we go to the Gentiles."
- In Acts 28:27-28   Paul announces to the "chief of the Jews" (Verse 17) who visited him in his Roman prison that "the salvation of God is gone to the Gentiles and they will hear it."

Daniel 1:3-4

"³ And the king spake unto Ashpenaz the master of his eunuchs, that he should bring *certain* of the children of Israel, and of the king's seed, and of the princes; ⁴ Children in whom *was* no blemish, but well favoured, and skilful in all wisdom, and cunning in knowledge, and understanding science, and such as *had* ability in them to stand in the king's palace, and whom they might teach the learning and the tongue of the Chaldeans." (Dan 1:3-4)

Nebuchadnezzar wanted to tap into the wisdom of the countries that he had conquered. The science of the orient in those days was the top science of the day. Nebuchadnezzar (though a heathen) was a wise king. He wanted to surround himself with wise counsel – not only from his own land but from other lands and cultures as well.

We meet Daniel, Hananiah, Mishael, and Azariah:

Daniel 1:5-7

⁵ And the king appointed them a daily provision of the king's meat, and of the wine which he drank: so nourishing them three years, that at the end thereof they might stand before the king. ⁶ Now among these were of the children of Judah, Daniel, Hananiah, Mishael, and Azariah: ⁷ Unto whom the prince of the eunuchs gave names: for he gave unto Daniel *the name* of Belteshazzar; and to Hananiah, of Shadrach; and to Mishael, of Meshach; and to Azariah, of Abednego.

The name Daniel means "God is my Judge". The name Belteshazzer means "Prince with Baal". The change in Daniel's name is part of the effort of the heathen king to change the character, destiny and direction in lives of the children. This is an example of what the world tries to do in the lives of children today (Romans 12:1-2). Baal worship is, in reality, the worship of the devil. We will be seeing a contest being played out in the Book of Daniel between God and the Devil.

Daniel 1: 8-16

⁸ But Daniel purposed in his heart that he would not defile himself with the portion of the king's meat, nor with the wine which he drank: therefore he requested of the prince of the eunuchs that he might not defile himself. ⁹ Now God had brought Daniel into favour and tender love with the prince of the eunuchs. ¹⁰ And the prince of the eunuchs said unto Daniel, I fear my lord the king, who hath appointed your meat and your drink: for why should he see your faces worse liking than the children which *are* of your sort? then shall ye make *me* endanger my head to the king. ¹¹ Then said Daniel to Melzar, whom the prince of the eunuchs had set over Daniel, Hananiah, Mishael, and Azariah, ¹² Prove thy servants, I beseech thee, ten days; and let them give us pulse to eat, and water to drink. ¹³ Then let our countenances be looked upon before thee, and the countenance of the children that eat of the portion of the king's meat: and as thou seest, deal with thy servants. ¹⁴ So he consented to them in this matter, and proved them ten days. ¹⁵ And at the end of ten days their countenances

appeared fairer and fatter in flesh than all the children which did eat the portion of the king's meat. [16] Thus Melzar took away the portion of their meat, and the wine that they should drink; and gave them pulse.

God had special dietary requirements for Israel (Lev. 11:44-47). It is likely that Daniel was also a Nasserite and would not drink wine (Num. 6:3). While we today are free from these requirements (1Cor. 8:8; 10:25-27), it was a serious matter for these children to defile themselves with the heathen diet (Exodus 34:13 & 14). Note that the unclean thing in 1Corinthians 6:14-17 is idolatry. Daniel and his friends therefore purposed in their hearts to not defile themselves with the king's food, not only for the sake of the Law of Moses being against it but also in that it had been offered to idols.

Daniel 1:17 – 20

[17] As for these four children, God gave them knowledge and skill in all learning and wisdom: and Daniel had understanding in all visions and dreams. [18] Now at the end of the days that the king had said he should bring them in, then the prince of the eunuchs brought them in before Nebuchadnezzar. [19] And the king communed with them; and among them all was found none like Daniel, Hananiah, Mishael, and Azariah: therefore stood they before the king. [20] And in all matters of wisdom *and* understanding, that the king enquired of them, he found them ten times better than all the magicians *and* astrologers that *were* in all his realm.

This should be an encouragement to the believer today that the wisdom of God is wiser than men and that "…we have received not the spirit of the world, but the spirit which is of God, that we might know the things that are freely given to us of God." (1Cor. 2:12) Then as today, God gives wisdom, knowledge, and understanding to the humble believer who truly fears Him. These children did shine when they stood before the king. Note they were ten times better than all of the magicians and astrologers. Psalm 3:1-5 explains why: "[1] My son, forget not my law; but let thine heart keep my commandments: [2] For length of days, and long life, and peace, shall they add to thee. [3] Let not mercy and truth forsake thee: bind them about thy neck; write them upon the table of thine heart: [4] So shalt thou find favour and good understanding in the sight of God and man. [5] Trust in the LORD with all thine heart; and lean not unto thine own understanding. [6] In all thy ways acknowledge him, and he shall direct thy paths."

Daniel 1:21

[21] And Daniel continued *even* unto the first year of king Cyrus.

This covers a period of 70 plus years. Daniel was there in Babylon for most of the period of the captivity. He was in Susa (the capital of the Persian Empire) during the reign of the Medes and the Persians.

Daniel Chapter 1: Study Guide Questions

1. List the three Bible passages that describe the captivity of the last three kings of Israel.

2. List the three step failure of Israel in the New Testament;

3. List the three step departure of God's glory from the Temple in Ezekiel.

4. List the three step departure of Christ from the Temple.

5. List the three step process of God's turning to the Gentiles in the book of Acts.

Chapter 2
The Dream of the Great Image
An Overview of the Times of the Gentiles

Daniel 2:1

¹ And in the second year of the reign of Nebuchadnezzar Nebuchadnezzar dreamed dreams, wherewith his spirit was troubled, and his sleep brake from him.

Here we have the king dreaming a dream that troubled him. He understands that it is not an ordinary dream and seeks wisdom from his wise men to give him understanding of it. He is a typical man of the world who is looking for wisdom but looking for it in the wrong place.

Daniel 2:2

² Then the king commanded to call the magicians, and the astrologers, and the sorcerers, and the Chaldeans, for to shew the king his dreams. So they came and stood before the king.

Magicians were a group that used black magic. The astrologers were a group that looked for wisdom in the stars. The wise men of Matthew 2:1-2 who came asking "Where is he that is born the King of the Jews?" were their descendents. The sorcerers were a group that sought to communicate with the dead for wisdom. The Chaldeans were the philosophers and scientists who sought for wisdom in the academics of the human race. However, the Bible believer knows real wisdom because he has found it in the only source of true wisdom – that being the Word of God.

Daniel 2:3-6

³ And the king said unto them, I have dreamed a dream, and my spirit was troubled to know the dream. ⁴ Then spake the Chaldeans to the king in Syriack, O king, live for ever: tell thy servants the dream, and we will shew the interpretation. ⁵ The king answered and said to the Chaldeans, The thing is gone from me: if ye will not make known unto me the dream, with the interpretation thereof, ye shall be cut in pieces, and your houses shall be made a dunghill. ⁶ But if ye shew the dream, and the interpretation thereof, ye shall receive of me gifts and rewards and great honour: therefore shew me the dream, and the interpretation thereof.

We do not know for certain if the dream is truly forgotten. One thing the king will find out is if these wise men have true wisdom from a deity or not.

Daniel 2:7-9

⁷ They answered again and said, Let the king tell his servants the dream, and we will shew the interpretation of it. ⁸ The king answered and said, I know of certainty that ye would gain the time, because ye see the thing is gone from me. ⁹ But if ye will not make known unto me the dream, *there is but* one decree for you: for ye have prepared lying and corrupt words to speak before me, till the time be changed: therefore tell me the dream, and I shall know that ye can shew me the interpretation thereof.

Here again, we see the wisdom of the king. Likely he suspected that they were pulling his leg and had been doing so for a long time, but here he puts them to the test.

Daniel 2:10-11

[10] The Chaldeans answered before the king, and said, There is not a man upon the earth that can shew the king's matter: therefore *there is* no king, lord, nor ruler, *that* asked such things at any magician, or astrologer, or Chaldean. [11] And *it is* a rare thing that the king requireth, and there is none other that can shew it before the king, except the gods, whose dwelling is not with flesh.

Here the Chaldeans are compelled to admit that they were frauds when it comes to having wisdom that can actually solve real problems. We see that in the world around us today. The farther men drift from the Word of God, the more apparent their foolishness becomes evident. We see the failure of religion (religious systems) to help people when they have a real need for truth. Religion has nothing to offer but emptiness. However, true spiritually has true wisdom to offer to the world because it comes from the mind of Christ (1Cor. 2:16).

Daniel 2:12-14

[12] For this cause the king was angry and very furious, and commanded to destroy all the wise *men* of Babylon. [13] And the decree went forth that the wise *men* should be slain; and they sought Daniel and his fellows to be slain. [14] Then Daniel answered with counsel and wisdom to Arioch the captain of the king's guard, which was gone forth to slay the wise *men* of Babylon:

Here we see Daniel's wisdom, patience and gentleness. The believer need not be in a hurry when he trusts in the Lord and waits on the Lord (Philippians 4:2-8).

Daniel 2:15-16

[15] He answered and said to Arioch the king's captain, Why *is* the decree *so* hasty from the king? Then Arioch made the thing known to Daniel. [16] Then Daniel went in, and desired of the king that he would give him time, and that he would shew the king the interpretation.

Daniel's faith and his wisdom are evident here as he asks for time to consult with the Lord. The believer does not have to have anxiety for anything if he will simply take all matters that would trouble him to the Lord in prayer, supplication, with thanksgiving and then searches the Word for answers.

Daniel 2:17-18

[17] Then Daniel went to his house, and made the thing known to Hananiah, Mishael, and Azariah, his companions: [18] That they would desire mercies of the God of heaven concerning this secret; that Daniel and his fellows should not perish with the rest of the wise *men* of Babylon.

Here we see Daniel's resource – prayer to God. Daniel's concern was for these godly men of Israel. He was not too unduly concerned about the fraudulent wise men of Babylon, though they too benefitted by the fact that there was a man of God in their midst.

Daniel 2:19

¹⁹ Then was the secret revealed unto Daniel in a night vision. Then Daniel blessed the God of heaven.

Here we see Daniel give the credit to the one who has the real wisdom – the God of heaven. God revealed a secret to Daniel here. We today do not look for any secrets to be revealed to us because all of the secrets that God would have us know have been revealed in the Word of God. We go in prayer to the Word of God for our answers today because there, in the completed Word of God, do we find all of the answers to our questions that render us fully equipped for every good work (2Tim. 3:16).

Daniel 2:20-23

²⁰ Daniel answered and said, Blessed be the name of God for ever and ever: for wisdom and might are his: ²¹ And he changeth the times and the seasons: he removeth kings, and setteth up kings: he giveth wisdom unto the wise, and knowledge to them that know understanding: ²² He revealeth the deep and secret things: he knoweth what *is* in the darkness, and the light dwelleth with him. ²³ I thank thee, and praise thee, O thou God of my fathers, who hast given me wisdom and might, and hast made known unto me now what we desired of thee: for thou hast *now* made known unto us the king's matter.

Here again Daniel gives credit to the God of heaven. Here we see Daniel's worship – He attributes all worth to God. Note his prayer of thanksgiving:
- God's name is blessed.
- Wisdom and might are His.
- He changes seasons and times.
- He removes and sets up kings.
- He gives wisdom to the wise.
- He gives knowledge to them that understand.
- He reveals the secret things.
- He knowest what is in the darkness and light dwelleth with him.

Daniel Comes to the Rescue

Daniel 2:24-25

²⁴ Therefore Daniel went in unto Arioch, whom the king had ordained to destroy the wise *men* of Babylon: he went and said thus unto him; Destroy not the wise *men* of Babylon: bring me in before the king, and I will shew unto the king the interpretation. ²⁵ Then Arioch brought in Daniel before the king in haste, and said thus unto him, I have found a man of the captives of Judah, that will make known unto the king the interpretation.

The wise men of Babylon were saved because there was a man of God in their midst (c.f. Acts 27:22-44). Let it be that men around us might be saved because there was a man of God (we as believers) in their midst. Daniel was a means of salvation for these Gentiles. Israel was to be that for the Gentiles. We (members of the Body of Christ) today are to be the means of salvation for the world around us today.

Daniel directs the King's thoughts to God

Daniel 2:26-28

 [26] The king answered and said to Daniel, whose name *was* Belteshazzar, Art thou able to make known unto me the dream which I have seen, and the interpretation thereof? [27] Daniel answered in the presence of the king, and said, The secret which the king hath demanded cannot the wise *men*, the astrologers, the magicians, the soothsayers, shew unto the king; [28] But there is a God in heaven that revealeth secrets, and maketh known to the king Nebuchadnezzar what shall be in the latter days. Thy dream, and the visions of thy head upon thy bed, are these; …

This is our work today as well – to direct people to the Word of God for the truth and the answer to their questions. Daniel was a source of light to this king. We are that light to our world today. Light is that which comes to us with regeneration. We as believers were once darkness but now, as regenerated people (saints) we are light in the Lord (Eph. 5:8-14). That light gives us the ability to see through the darkness to discern the spiritual reality of what is around us.

Ephesians 5:8-14 [8] For ye were sometimes darkness, but now *are ye* light in the Lord: walk as children of light: [9] (For the fruit of the Spirit *is* in all goodness and righteousness and truth;) [10] Proving what is acceptable unto the Lord. [11] And have no fellowship with the unfruitful works of darkness, but rather reprove *them*. [12] For it is a shame even to speak of those things which are done of them in secret. [13] But all things that are reproved are made manifest by the light: for whatsoever doth make manifest is light. [14] Wherefore he saith, Awake thou that sleepest, and arise from the dead, and Christ shall give thee light.

Daniel 2:29

[29] As for thee, O king, thy thoughts came *into thy mind* upon thy bed, what should come to pass hereafter: and he that revealeth secrets maketh known to thee what shall come to pass.

This is what prophecy is all about – making known what shall be hereafter. God, who exists outside of the space-matter-time continuum has the ability to see what man will do as free-moral-agents, acts to ensure that His eternal purposes are secure, while allowing man to act of his own free will and then hold man accountable to Him for man's actions.

Daniel credits his wisdom to God, the real source of wisdom

Daniel 2:30-36

[30] But as for me, this secret is not revealed to me for *any* wisdom that I have more than any living, but for *their* sakes that shall make known the interpretation to the king, and that thou mightest know the thoughts of thy heart. [31] Thou, O king, sawest, and behold a great image. This great image, whose brightness *was* excellent, stood before thee; and the form thereof *was* terrible. [32] This image's head *was* of fine gold, his breast and his arms of silver, his belly and his thighs of brass, [33] His legs of iron, his feet part of iron and part of clay. [34] Thou sawest till that a stone was cut out without hands, which smote the image upon his feet *that were* of iron and clay, and brake them to pieces. [35] Then was the iron, the clay, the brass, the silver, and the gold, broken to pieces together, and became

like the chaff of the summer threshingfloors; and the wind carried them away, that no place was found for them: and the stone that smote the image became a great mountain, and filled the whole earth. [36] This *is* the dream; and we will tell the interpretation thereof before the king.

Daniel gives the exact details of the dream and then goes on to give the interpretation of it. What the king is viewing in the dream (the vision) is a prewritten history of the Gentile dominion of the earth, from that time forward, until the Lord God of Israel sets up His kingdom on earth.

A Millennium of prewritten history in three verses

Daniel 2: 37-40

[37] Thou, O king, *art* a king of kings: for the God of heaven hath given thee a kingdom, power, and strength, and glory. [38] And wheresoever the children of men dwell, the beasts of the field and the fowls of the heaven hath he given into thine hand, and hath made thee ruler over them all. Thou *art* this head of gold. [39] And after thee shall arise another kingdom inferior to thee, and another third kingdom of brass, which shall bear rule over all the earth. [40] And the fourth kingdom shall be strong as iron: forasmuch as iron breaketh in pieces and subdueth all *things*: and as iron that breaketh all these, shall it break in pieces and bruise.

Here Daniel goes on to interpret the dream. The head of gold represents Nebuchadnezzar. The first king of Babylon was Nimrod (Gen. 10:5-10). The Gentiles were dispersed around the globe as a result of Nimrod's actions. Nebuchadnezzar is the first king to start the times of the Gentiles during which Gentile kings seek to undo God's work of disrupting the globalism of Babel. The great image is presenting a sequentially progressive unfolding of the kingdoms that constitute the times of the Gentiles until the kingdom is returned to Israel under the reign of her Messiah. The prophet Jeremiah foretold of this captivity under the king of Babylon.

Jeremiah's Prophecy

"[5] I have made the earth, the man and the beast that *are* upon the ground, by my great power and by my outstretched arm, and have given it unto whom it seemed meet unto me. [6] And now have I given all these lands into the hand of Nebuchadnezzar the king of Babylon, my servant; and the beasts of the field have I given him also to serve him. [7] And all nations shall serve him, and his son, and his son's son, until the very time of his land come: and then many nations and great kings shall serve themselves of him. [8] And it shall come to pass, *that* the nation and kingdom which will not serve the same Nebuchadnezzar the king of Babylon, and that will not put their neck under the yoke of the king of Babylon, that nation will I punish, saith the LORD, with the sword, and with the famine, and with the pestilence, until I have consumed them by his hand. [9] Therefore hearken not ye to your prophets, nor to your diviners, nor to your dreamers, nor to your enchanters, nor to your sorcerers, which speak unto you, saying, Ye shall not serve the king of Babylon:" (Jeremiah 27:5-9)

In Jeremiah 36:9 Jeremiah was instructed by God to write to Jehoiakim why the crown would be taken from Israel. In Jeremiah 36:22-26, Jehoiakim reads the scroll and burns it. In Jeremiah 36:27-30, The Lord tells Jeremiah to write it again and add to it that "…He [Jehoiakim] shall have none to sit upon the throne of

David…" Zedekiah the brother of Jehoiakim was made king instead of Jehoiakim but his sons were slain before him (2Kings 25:7; Jer. 29:21; 39:6; and 52:10).

There is an important and interesting point to be made of the genealogy of the Savior in Matthew's Gospel Chapter 1 verses 2-16. In verse 11 we find the godly king Josiah being the father of Jechonias (Jehoiakim) who is the father of Jehoiachin (Coniah) of whom the Lord said that no man of his seed will sit on the throne of David (Jer. 22:24-30). Joseph is of Coniah's seed but he is not the physical father of Jesus. The fact that Joseph is the husband of Mary enables Christ to sit on the throne of David as the seed of David by marriage of Mary to Joseph. Christ is the seed of David through the royal seed line through Solomon by the fact that Mary is the wife of Joseph. He is also of the seed of David through Mary through another son of David – Nathan (Luke 3:31). Christ had to be the virgin born son of David through a different lineage than Joseph's in order for Him to sit on the throne of David.

This great image represents the entire duration of the times of the Gentiles. It began about the year 606 BC. The head of gold represents Nebuchadnezzar's kingdom. That was followed in about 536 BC with the next kingdom to hold sway over Israel – The kingdom of the Medes and Persians. The second kingdom is represented by the arms of silver. We will see in Chapter 5 Verses 25-31 that this kingdom that is represented by the arms of silver comprises what is today the country of Iran. The third Gentile power to rule over the throne of Israel is the kingdom of Alexander of Greece (represented by the belly and thighs of brass). This happened about 330 BC. We will see this kingdom described in Daniel 8:20 & 21. The fourth kingdom is (like the second) in two parts as represented by the legs of iron. Identifying the fourth kingdom is a bit more difficult than it is to identify the first three. Some suggest that it would be the Roman Empire in that the Roman Empire ruled Israel during the time of the Lord's earthly ministry. The Roman Empire was in two parts (eastern and western) but that division did not happen until about the seventh century AD. The fourth empire grew out of the third (the Greek). The Greek empire was divided into four kingdoms (Dan. 8:22). However, three of those become reunited again as the Roman Empire. The two fold division then is the three together and the one. These ultimately are the king of the north (the king of Assyria) and the king of the south (the king of Egypt) as they show up during the end times. We will see the conflict between the two in Daniel 11 during the end times. Out of one of these will come the "king of fierce countenance" (Dan. 8:23) who will be the antichrist.

Daniel 2:41-43

[41] And whereas thou sawest the feet and toes, part of potters' clay, and part of iron, the kingdom shall be divided; but there shall be in it of the strength of the iron, forasmuch as thou sawest the iron mixed with miry clay. [42] And *as* the toes of the feet *were* part of iron, and part of clay, *so* the kingdom shall be partly strong, and partly broken. [43] And whereas thou sawest iron mixed with miry clay, they shall mingle themselves with the seed of men: but they shall not cleave one to another, even as iron is not mixed with clay.

These feet are very interesting. They are of clay. Adam was made of clay. Iron, on the other hand, is representative of the giants that were the result of the intermarriage of angels and the daughters of men as we find it in Genesis 6:2-4 cf. Deuteronomy 3:11 and 1Samuel 17:7 . The clay then would represent a time when there would be no strong kingdoms ruling over Israel. You might think of the clay as representing the rise of democratic forms of government as we have in the world today.

This story is all about Israel. From the time that Titus of Rome destroyed Jerusalem (about 70 AD) there was no rulership over Israel by a strong Gentile nation (Dan. 9:26). The ten toes are ten kings that will be on earth in the last days just before and during the time when the Lord returns. We note though that the toes are of iron and that the iron does not mix with the clay. We note too that "they [i.e. the ten toes] shall mingle themselves with the seed of men…" but "…that they shall not cleave one to another, even as the iron is not mixed with clay." Obviously these kings are not normal human beings, but are somehow demonic. We will encounter the ten toes of Daniel 2:44 again later. They are the ten horns of Daniel 7:24 and the ten kings of Revelation 17:12.

Daniel 2: 44-45

[44] And in the days of these kings shall the God of heaven set up a kingdom, which shall never be destroyed: and the kingdom shall not be left to other people, *but* it shall break in pieces and consume all these kingdoms, and it shall stand for ever. [45] Forasmuch as thou sawest that the stone was cut out of the mountain without hands, and that it brake in pieces the iron, the brass, the clay, the silver, and the gold; the great God hath made known to the king what shall come to pass hereafter: and the dream *is* certain, and the interpretation thereof sure.

It will be in the days of these kings represented by the ten toes that the God of heaven sets up His kingdom on earth to reclaim planet earth back to Himself. The stone is Christ. He is the true rock (Deut. 32:30-37). We see Him presented as the rock often in Scripture (1Cor. 10:4; Matt. 21:42-44; 1Peter 2:3-9).

Daniel 2:46-49

[46] Then the king Nebuchadnezzar fell upon his face, and worshipped Daniel, and commanded that they should offer an oblation and sweet odours unto him. [47] The king answered unto Daniel, and said, Of a truth *it is*, that your God *is* a God of gods, and a Lord of kings, and a revealer of secrets, seeing thou couldest reveal this secret. [48] Then the king made Daniel a great man, and gave him many great gifts, and made him ruler over the whole province of Babylon, and chief of the governors over all the wise *men* of Babylon. [49] Then Daniel requested of the king, and he set Shadrach, Meshach, and Abednego, over the affairs of the province of Babylon: but Daniel *sat* in the gate of the king.

To worship is to attribute worth to someone or something. Daniel shunned such attention but directed the glory to God. The king was converted to recognizing that the God, who Daniel served, is truly "a God of gods…" He will later in the book be further converted to faith in the God of Israel. Daniel then became essentially the second in command of the Babylonian kingdom with Shadrach, Meshach, and Abednego as ministers over the affairs of the province.

Here again we see Daniel take advantage of the opportunity to influence the kingdom for God. God is using Daniel to do what Israel, as a nation, was supposed to do when in the land of Israel – making known to the Gentiles the one true God. That is also what we are supposed to be doing as members of the church, which is Christ's body in the world today.

Daniel Chapter 2: Study Guide Questions

1. List the three groups of wise men that Nebuchadnezzar trusted in for wisdom.

2. How did Nebuchadnezzar demonstrate wisdom in Verses 3-9?

3. What was it that the wise men of Babylon were admitting in Verses 10 and 11?

4. How did Daniel demonstrate wisdom in verses 12-14?

5. Can we today expect an answer to our prayers in the manner that Daniel did in Verse 19? Why not?

6. To whom does Daniel give the credit in Verses 20 – 23?

7. According to Verse 28, God reveals secrets. Are there secrets that God has that He reveals today? Is God holding back secrets today? Where do we find the revelation of the secrets that God revealed?

8. What, according to Verse 29, is prophecy given for?

9. How many kings (kingdoms) will follow each other according to Verses 37 – 40?

10. Nimrod was the first king of Babel but why the focus on Nebuchadnezzar here in Verses 37 – 40?

11. What does the great image of Chapter 2 represent in history?

12. Ten horns, ten kings, ten toes, and miry clay; what do each represent?

13. What is significance of the stone being cut "without hands" in Verse 45?

14. What lesson did Nebuchadnezzar learn in Verse 46 – 49?

15. Whose work was it that gave Daniel broad influence in the world in his day?

Chapter 3
Nebuchadnezzar's Image and the Fiery Furnace

Daniel 3:1 (KJV)

[1] Nebuchadnezzar the king made an image of gold, whose height *was* threescore cubits, *and* the breadth thereof six cubits: he set it up in the plain of Dura, in the province of Babylon.

Here we see Nebuchadnezzar make an image of gold. As we think of the image of gold, we think of Daniel 2:38 where we find that the image in Nebuchadnezzar's dream had a head of gold, and that the interpretation was that he was that head of gold. Here we see him making an image of gold. It appears that the whole thing went to his head. He proceeds to make an image of himself entirely of gold.

In Revelation 13:1-15 we see the false prophet making an image to the antichrist. The false prophet then has power to do miracles such that he can call forth fire from heaven and to give what appears to be life to the image of the beast. He does as Nebuchadnezzar did and command everyone to bow down to the image.

This thing that we see in Daniel Chapter 3 is pure idolatry. However, the Bible presents an image of God in the person of Jesus Christ who is in fact the image of the invisible God. He (our Lord Jesus Christ) is the image of the invisible God (Col. 1:15) in that He is God manifest in the flesh as a man. As we study Him in scripture, we are changed into the image of Christ (2Cor. 4:6) so as to conform us to the image of His Son (Romans 8:29). "[17] Now the Lord is that Spirit: and where the Spirit of the Lord *is*, there *is* liberty. [18] But we all, with open face beholding as in a glass the glory of the Lord, are changed into the same image from glory to glory, *even* as by the Spirit of the Lord." (2Cor. 3:17-18)

Daniel 3:2-7

[2] Then Nebuchadnezzar the king sent to gather together the princes, the governors, and the captains, the judges, the treasurers, the counselors, the sheriffs, and all the rulers of the provinces, to come to the dedication of the image which Nebuchadnezzar the king had set up. [3] Then the princes, the governors, and captains, the judges, the treasurers, the counsellors, the sheriffs, and all the rulers of the provinces, were gathered together unto the dedication of the image that Nebuchadnezzar the king had set up; and they stood before the image that Nebuchadnezzar had set up. [4] Then an herald cried aloud, To you it is commanded, O people, nations, and languages, [5] *That* at what time ye hear the sound of the cornet, flute, harp, sackbut, psaltery, dulcimer, and all kinds of musick, ye fall down and worship the golden image that Nebuchadnezzar the king hath set up: [6] And whoso falleth not down and worshippeth shall the same hour be cast into the midst of a burning fiery furnace. [7] Therefore at that time, when all the people heard the sound of the cornet, flute, harp, sackbut, psaltery, and all kinds of musick, all the people, the nations, and the languages, fell down *and* worshipped the golden image that Nebuchadnezzar the king had set up.

Here Vverses 2 through 7 we find what the basis of dead religion is. The object of worship is a dead image. The worship service includes music to set the mood. Satan is a master musician in that he had musical instruments built into his very being (Ezekiel 28:11-16). The sons of God in the angelic world were musicians as well (Job 38:1-7). Satan knows how to use music to accomplish his objective of directing worship away from the true God to the images that he sets up. In Genesis 4:16-22 we see Cain's descendents develop music as a culture. The drug-sex-rebellion culture of today uses music to get control of the minds of young people. What we see here is an effort to make a one world religion and a one world government. What we see in Daniel is what a government run religion would look like. This is what started in Babel where there was a one world government, a one world language, and a one world religion (Gen. 11:1, 4). Ever since the confusion of tongues at Babel, man has been seeking to re-establish what was lost to man at Babel. The worship of the golden calf in Exodus 32:1-25 was based on music. Though music is misused as it is here, there is nonetheless a proper use of music (Eph 5:18-19; Col 3:16).

Daniel 3:8-12

[8] Wherefore at that time certain Chaldeans came near, and accused the Jews. [9] They spake and said to the king Nebuchadnezzar, O king, live for ever. [10] Thou, O king, hast made a decree, that every man that shall hear the sound of the cornet, flute, harp, sackbut, psaltery, and dulcimer, and all kinds of musick, shall fall down and worship the golden image: [11] And whoso falleth not down and worshippeth, *that* he should be cast into the midst of a burning fiery furnace. [12] There are certain Jews whom thou hast set over the affairs of the province of Babylon, Shadrach, Meshach, and Abednego; these men, O king, have not regarded thee: they serve not thy gods, nor worship the golden image which thou hast set up.

Here is true faithfulness in action. This is a typical case of the faithful remnant who will not compromise the truth.

Daniel 3:13-15

[13] Then Nebuchadnezzar in *his* rage and fury commanded to bring Shadrach, Meshach, and Abednego. Then they brought these men before the king. [14] Nebuchadnezzar spake and said unto them, *Is it* true, O Shadrach, Meshach, and Abednego, do not ye serve my gods, nor worship the golden image which I have set up? [15] Now if ye be ready that at what time ye hear the sound of the cornet, flute, harp, sackbut, psaltery, and dulcimer, and all kinds of musick, ye fall down and worship the image which I have made; *well*: but if ye worship not, ye shall be cast the same hour into the midst of a burning fiery furnace; and who *is* that God that shall deliver you out of my hands?

Here Nebuchadnezzar is furious that these children would not worship the image or his gods. He again gives them another opportunity to conform. This reminds us of the apostle's exhortation to believers to be not conformed to this world but to be transformed by the renewing of the mind so as to prove (literally to document for the world to see) what is the Lord's will for us.

Daniel 3:16-18

[16] Shadrach, Meshach, and Abednego, answered and said to the king, O Nebuchadnezzar, we *are* not careful to answer thee in this matter. [17] If it be *so*, our God whom we serve is able to deliver us from the burning fiery furnace, and he will deliver *us* out of thine hand, O king. [18] But if not, be it known unto thee, O king, that we will not serve thy gods, nor worship the golden image which thou hast set up.

These boys are ready and quick to give their answer to the king. They tell him in no uncertain terms that they will not worship his image or his gods. These boys will be examples to the tribulation saints who will be faced with the temptation to worship the beast and his image (Rev. 13:15). They loved not their lives unto death. That is what will be required of those in the tribulation period (Rev. 12:11).

Daniel 3:19-26

[19] Then was Nebuchadnezzar full of fury, and the form of his visage was changed against Shadrach, Meshach, and Abednego: *therefore* he spake, and commanded that they should heat the furnace one seven times more than it was wont to be heated. [20] And he commanded the most mighty men that *were* in his army to bind Shadrach, Meshach, and Abednego, *and* to cast *them* into the burning fiery furnace. [21] Then these men were bound in their coats, their hosen, and their hats, and their *other* garments, and were cast into the midst of the burning fiery furnace. [22] Therefore because the king's commandment was urgent, and the furnace exceeding hot, the flame of the fire slew those men that took up Shadrach, Meshach, and Abednego. [23] And these three men, Shadrach, Meshach, and Abednego, fell down bound into the midst of the burning fiery furnace. [24] Then Nebuchadnezzar the king was astonied, and rose up in haste, *and* spake, and said unto his counsellors, Did not we cast three men bound into the midst of the fire? They answered and said unto the king, True, O king. [25] He answered and said, Lo, I see four men loose, walking in the midst of the fire, and they have no hurt; and the form of the fourth is like the Son of God. [26] Then Nebuchadnezzar came near to the mouth of the burning fiery furnace, *and* spake, and said, Shadrach, Meshach, and Abednego, ye servants of the most high God, come forth, and come *hither*. Then Shadrach, Meshach, and Abednego, came forth of the midst of the fire.

Here an angel of the Lord delivered the three boys from the fire. The fire has no effect on them though it totally burned up the men who threw them into the furnace. Just as God was with the three boys to take them through the ordeal of the furnace, so He will be with Israel to take them through the ordeal of the tribulation (Isa. 43:1-2). This is what the apostle prophecies in Romans 11:26-27 "[26] And so all Israel shall be saved: as it is written, There shall come out of Sion the Deliverer, and shall turn away ungodliness from Jacob: [27] For this *is* my covenant unto them, when I shall take away their sins."

Daniel 3:27-29

[27] And the princes, governors, and captains, and the king's counselors, being gathered together, saw these men, upon whose bodies the fire had no power, nor was an hair of their head singed, neither were their coats changed, nor the smell of fire had passed on them. [28] *Then* Nebuchadnezzar spake, and said, Blessed *be* the God of Shadrach, Meshach, and Abednego, who hath sent his angel, and delivered his servants that trusted in him, and have changed the king's word, and yielded their bodies, that they might not serve nor worship any god, except their own God. [29] Therefore I make a decree, That every people, nation, and language, which speak any thing amiss against the God of Shadrach, Meshach, and Abednego, shall be cut in pieces, and their houses shall be made a dunghill: because there is no other God that can deliver after this sort.

The first king of the times of the Gentiles (Nebuchadnezzar) learns that the God of Israel is the true God and that He can and will deliver Israel. He is not converted yet to total faith in the God of Israel, yet (as we will see later).However he is starting to take note that the God of Israel is different from his gods. Here again God is honored through the work of faithful Israelites – though they be but a few of all of those that comprise the nation.

Daniel 3: 30

³⁰ Then the king promoted Shadrach, Meshach, and Abednego, in the province of Babylon.

The nation at large is not functioning in the world the way that God called the nation out to be. However, there are some faithful Jews who are in a position to be the influence in the world that the unfaithful nation can not yet be.

Daniel Chapter 3: Study Guide Questions

1. What comparison do we see between the image of Daniel 3 and Revelation 13?

2. How does the passage in Verses 2-9 epitomize dead religion?

3. What does Verse 15 tell us about Nebuchadnezzar's impression of Israel's God?

4. The three boys in Verses 16 & 17 are a type of whom in the coming tribulation period?

5. Was their faith in deliverance from the fire or was it faith in God in spite of the fire?

6. In what world did the three boys' faithfulness put them into a position of power and authority?

Chapter 4
Nebuchadnezzar's Tree Vision and His Insanity

Daniel 4:1-3

[1] Nebuchadnezzar the king, unto all people, nations, and languages, that dwell in all the earth; Peace be multiplied unto you. [2] I thought it good to shew the signs and wonders that the high God hath wrought toward me. [3] How great *are* his signs! And how mighty *are* his wonders! His kingdom *is* an everlasting kingdom, and his dominion *is* from generation to generation.

This account is by Nebuchadnezzar himself. It speaks of his conversion to belief in the God of heaven. This conversion is a type of the conversion that the Gentile nations will have as a result of the seventieth week of Daniel Chapter 9 – i.e. the tribulation period. Just as Nebuchadnezzar goes insane under the influence of this own power and might, so the Gentiles will be insane under the influence of the antichrist.

Daniel 4:4-9

[4] I Nebuchadnezzar was at rest in mine house, and flourishing in my palace: [5] I saw a dream which made me afraid, and the thoughts upon my bed and the visions of my head troubled me. [6] Therefore made I a decree to bring in all the wise *men* of Babylon before me, that they might make known unto me the interpretation of the dream. [7] Then came in the magicians, the astrologers, the Chaldeans, and the soothsayers: and I told the dream before them; but they did not make known unto me the interpretation thereof. [8] But at the last Daniel came in before me, whose name *was* Belteshazzar, according to the name of my god, and in whom *is* the spirit of the holy gods: and before him I told the dream, *saying,* [9] O Belteshazzar, master of the magicians, because I know that the spirit of the holy gods *is* in thee, and no secret troubleth thee, tell me the visions of my dream that I have seen, and the interpretation thereof.

It must be remembered that the decree that Nebuchadnezzar is making in the first three verses is the decree that he made in Chapter 3:29 as a result of him being impressed with the power of the God of the three Hebrew children. However, he is not yet converted to the true God yet. We see this here in Verse 8 in that that he still trusts in his god (i.e. Baal). In Verse 4 we see him enjoying peace and prosperity. As such, he does as many do – remain indifferent to the fact that there is a true God to whom they will give an account. While enjoying such peace and prosperity, he has no interest in exploring other alternatives. However, he has another dream that troubles him. His first tack is to trust in his own wise men that are trusting in his god but quickly realizes that they have no answers for him. He then turns, as a last resort, to the one who helped him before – Daniel. We see from Verse 18 that the king trusts in Daniel.

Nebuchadnezzar's Dream

Daniel 4:10-17

[10] Thus *were* the visions of mine head in my bed; I saw, and behold a tree in the midst of the earth, and the height thereof *was* great. [11] The tree grew, and was strong, and the height thereof reached unto heaven, and the sight thereof to the end of all the earth: [12] The leaves thereof *were* fair, and the fruit thereof much, and in it *was* meat for all: the beasts of the field had shadow under it, and the

fowls of the heaven dwelt in the boughs thereof, and all flesh was fed of it. [13] I saw in the visions of my head upon my bed, and, behold, a watcher and an holy one came down from heaven; [14] He cried aloud, and said thus, Hew down the tree, and cut off his branches, shake off his leaves, and scatter his fruit: let the beasts get away from under it, and the fowls from his branches: [15] Nevertheless leave the stump of his roots in the earth, even with a band of iron and brass, in the tender grass of the field; and let it be wet with the dew of heaven, and *let* his portion *be* with the beasts in the grass of the earth: [16] Let his heart be changed from man's, and let a beast's heart be given unto him; and let seven times pass over him. [17] This matter *is* by the decree of the watchers, and the demand by the word of the holy ones: to the intent that the living may know that the most High ruleth in the kingdom of men, and giveth it to whomsoever he will, and setteth up over it the basest of men.

The Dream:

- A tree in the earth grew to great height.(Verse 10)
- The height reached unto the heaven.
- The tree could be seen from the whole known earth (Verse 11).
- The tree had fair foliage and produced much fruit.
- It provided food for all ("…all flesh was fed of it…" – Verse 12).
- Beasts of the field found shade under it.
- Fowls of the haven dwelt in the boughs of it.
- A watcher and a holy one (cf. Deut. 33:2; Dan. 8:13; Zech. 14:56; Jude 14) come down from heaven (Verse 13).
- The watcher instructs others to cut the tree down and cut off its branches (cf Ezek. 31:1-4 of the Assyrian).
- The stump is to be left in the ground (Verse 15).
- Seven times are to pass over him (Verse 16). A time is often used in reference to a year in scripture. This gets one to thinking of some connection with the tribulation period which is seven years long.
- The decree is by the watchers (angels) and by the demand of the holy ones (elect angels Verse 17)
- The purpose of the dream is given in Verse 17: "…to the intent that the living may know that the most High ruleth in the kingdom of men, and giveth it to whomsoever he will, and setteth up over it the basest of men."

Nebuchadnezzar calls Daniel for an interpretation of the dream. He has learned from the experience in Chapter 2 that Daniel has the ability to do so because of his faithfulness to the true God.

Daniel 4:18-19

[18] This dream I king Nebuchadnezzar have seen. Now thou, O Belteshazzar, declare the interpretation thereof, forasmuch as all the wise *men* of my kingdom are not able to make known unto me the interpretation: but thou *art* able; for the spirit of the holy gods *is* in thee. [19] Then Daniel, whose name *was* Belteshazzar, was astonied for one hour, and his thoughts troubled him. The king spake, and said, Belteshazzar, let not the dream, or the interpretation thereof, trouble thee. Belteshazzar answered and said, My lord, the dream *be* to them that hate thee, and the interpretation thereof to thine enemies.

Daniel is overtaken in sadness for the king and can't talk of it for an hour. It is only after the king presses him that he gives the interpretation. The interpretation is good news -- not for him but for his enemies.

Daniel 4:20-22

[20] The tree that thou sawest, which grew, and was strong, whose height reached unto the heaven, and the sight thereof to all the earth; [21] Whose leaves *were* fair, and the fruit thereof much, and in it *was* meat for all; under which the beasts of the field dwelt, and upon whose branches the fowls of the heaven had their habitation: [22] It *is* thou, O king, that art grown and become strong: for thy greatness is grown, and reacheth unto heaven, and thy dominion to the end of the earth.

Here, like in the other dream (in Chapter 2) where Nebuchadnezzar was the head of gold, the tree represents him. This time however, it does not represent him in a positive or honorable way.

Daniel 4:23-25

[23] And whereas the king saw a watcher and an holy one coming down from heaven, and saying, Hew the tree down, and destroy it; yet leave the stump of the roots thereof in the earth, even with a band of iron and brass, in the tender grass of the field; and let it be wet with the dew of heaven, and *let* his portion *be* with the beasts of the field, till seven times pass over him; [24] This *is* the interpretation, O king, and this *is* the decree of the most High, which is come upon my lord the king: [25] That they shall drive thee from men, and thy dwelling shall be with the beasts of the field, and they shall make thee to eat grass as oxen, and they shall wet thee with the dew of heaven, and seven times shall pass over thee, till thou know that the most High ruleth in the kingdom of men, and giveth it to whomsoever he will.

In Verse 23, the king saw a "watcher and an holy one…" come down from heaven. A watcher is an angelic creature who is apparently charged with watching the activity in the king's life and is actually capable of acting to influence the affairs of men as was done here. A point of doctrine is in order here regarding angelic intervention in the affairs of men. In Israel's program we find that angels are "…ministering spirits, sent forth to minister for them who shall be heirs of salvation." (Hebrews 1:7\&14) Today, in the dispensation of the grace of God, angels are observing what the Holy Spirit is doing in the lives of believers. However, rather than intervening, they are actually learning about the wisdom of God as they observe God's grace produce righteous conduct in the lives of believers.

We mortal men think that we live private lives and yet (as here) our actions are observed and noted. There is a lesson for us to learn from this. That lesson is seen in Psalm 139:7-12 -- no one can escape the eye of the Spirit of God.

Nebuchadnezzar will be driven from civilization and will live with the beast of the field like an animal and they (angels?) shall make him eat grass and be wet him with the dew of heaven until seven times (cf. Dan. 7:35) pass over him. In the end, he will know that the most high (Gen. 14:18-22; Deut. 32:8; 2Sam. 22:14; Psalm 47:2; Isa. 14:14; Dan. 3:26; etc.) rules in the kingdoms of men and that God will set up whom He will in the kingdom of men. The term "the most high" is a reference to God as the one who owns both heaven and earth (Gen. 14:18-20).

Daniel 4:26

> [26] And whereas they commanded to leave the stump of the tree roots; thy kingdom shall be sure unto thee, after that thou shalt have known that the heavens do rule.

The kingdom will be given back to the king when he learns the lesson of verse 25. We saw from the first three verses that Nebuchadnezzar had learned that the God of Heaven is real. Now he must learn that what transpires on earth is under the rule of the God of heaven.

Daniel 4:27

> [27] Wherefore, O king, let my counsel be acceptable unto thee, and break off thy sins by righteousness, and thine iniquities by shewing mercy to the poor; if it may be a lengthening of thy tranquillity.

Daniel gave the king advice consistent with the law. This would be the repentance of a man under law as in Ezekiel 18:21. Daniel understood that the prophecy is sure but that he could lengthen his tranquility by repentance.

Daniel 4:28-31

> [28] All this came upon the king Nebuchadnezzar. [29] At the end of twelve months he walked in the palace of the kingdom of Babylon. [30] The king spake, and said, Is not this great Babylon, that I have built for the house of the kingdom by the might of my power, and for the honour of my majesty? [31] While the word *was* in the king's mouth, there fell a voice from heaven, *saying*, O king Nebuchadnezzar, to thee it is spoken; The kingdom is departed from thee.

Nebuchadnezzar had twelve months of tranquility but then his pride got the best of him. He no more than had the words of verse 30 out of his mouth that the kingdom was taken from him.

Daniel 4:32-33

> [32] And they shall drive thee from men, and thy dwelling *shall be* with the beasts of the field: they shall make thee to eat grass as oxen, and seven times shall pass over thee, until thou know that the most High ruleth in the kingdom of men, and giveth it to whomsoever he will. [33] The same hour was the thing fulfilled upon Nebuchadnezzar: and he was driven from men, and did eat grass as oxen, and his body was wet with the dew of heaven, till his hairs were grown like eagles' *feathers*, and his nails like birds' *claws*.

The words of the prophecy were fulfilled to the smallest detail.

Daniel 4:34-35

> [34] And at the end of the days I Nebuchadnezzar lifted up mine eyes unto heaven, and mine understanding returned unto me, and I blessed the most High, and I praised and honoured him that liveth for ever, whose dominion *is* an everlasting dominion, and his kingdom *is* from generation to generation: [35] And all the inhabitants of the earth *are* reputed as nothing: and he doeth according to

his will in the army of heaven, and *among* the inhabitants of the earth: and none can stay his hand, or say unto him, What doest thou?

Nebuchadnezzar not only acknowledges that the God of heaven rules in the affairs of men, but that He is an eternal God and that His dominion will be forever. After seven years, his reason returned to him but only after he learned that "…the Most High …doeth according to his will… and none can stay his hand…" He learned that the inhabitants of the earth are powerless to resist God's will and that God will give men the government that they deserve (Ezek. 14:1-4). We should note at this point that God, in the Old Testament scriptures, interceded directly in the affairs of men so as to intercede for His nation. It is different today. Today, God's interaction with man is of a spiritual nature whereby the Holy Spirit acts to accomplish redemption in people's lives, one by one, as individuals come in faith to the redeeming work of Christ on the Cross. The basic difference is that under His program with Israel, He dealt with Israel on the basis of covenants with a covenant people. Today he works in the lives of men on the basis of a body of doctrine called "the preaching of Jesus Christ according to the revelation of the mystery."

Daniel 4:36-37

[36] At the same time my reason returned unto me; and for the glory of my kingdom, mine honour and brightness returned unto me; and my counselors and my lords sought unto me; and I was established in my kingdom, and excellent majesty was added unto me. [37] Now I Nebuchadnezzar praise and extol and honour the King of heaven, all whose works *are* truth, and his ways judgment: and those that walk in pride he is able to abase.

This is the key lesson that Nebuchadnezzar (and all Gentile kings after him) had to learn "i.e. those that walk in pride he is able to abase." (Verse 37)

Daniel Chapter 4: Study Guide Questions

1. In Verses 1-3 we see the conversion of Nebuchadnezzar to belief in the one true God. What future conversion does this typify?

2. What happened to Nebuchadnezzar to prompt his conversion?

3. Did his conversion come when Daniel revealed the dream to him or did it come as a result of him having gone through the fulfillment of the dream?

4. What happened to him in Verses 16 and 25?

5. Who are the watchers of Verse 17?

6. According to Verse 25, when did Nebuchadnezzar's sanity return to him?

7. What advice did Daniel give to him in Verse 27?

8. How long did it take for the dream to be fulfilled? What triggered the fulfillment?

9. According to verse 34, what did Nebuchadnezzar turn to that brought him back to his right mind?

10. According to Verse 37, what was the lesson that Nebuchadnezzar took form this experience?

Chapter 5
Belshazzar's Pride and the Writing on the Wall

Daniel 5:1

¹ Belshazzar the king made a great feast to a thousand of his lords, and drank wine before the thousand.

We ask at this point "Who is Belshazzar?" Outside of this passage and other passages or extra-biblical literature he is nowhere to be found until the discovery of the Nabonidus Cylinder. Nebuchadnezzar's only son was Evil-merodach who we find referenced in 2Kings 25:27-29

"²⁶ And all the people, both small and great, and the captains of the armies, arose, and came to Egypt: for they were afraid of the Chaldees. ²⁷ And it came to pass in the seven and thirtieth year of the captivity of Jehoiachin king of Judah, in the twelfth month, on the seven and twentieth *day* of the month, *that* Evilmerodach king of Babylon in the year that he began to reign did lift up the head of Jehoiachin king of Judah out of prison; ²⁸ And he spake kindly to him, and set his throne above the throne of the kings that *were* with him in Babylon; ²⁹ And changed his prison garments: and he did eat bread continually before him all the days of his life." (2Kings 25:27-29)

At the death of Nebuchadnezzar, his son Evil-merodach succeeded him to the throne about 561 BC. However, Evil-merodach was murdered by Nergal-sharezer, the husband of one of Nebuchadnezzar's daughters who then ascended to the throne about 591 BC. He (Nergal-sharezer) in turn was murdered by Nabonidus, the husband of another of Nebuchadnezzar's daughters. Though Nabonidus ascended to the throne, his son Belshazzar actually reigned in Babylon as his coregent while Nabonidus was spending most of his time away from Babylon. Thus we have the prophecy of Jeremiah 27:7 which says of Nebuchadnezzar: "And all nations shall serve him, his son, and his son's son, until the very time of his land come…"

Belshazzar's Feast

Daniel 5:2-4

² Belshazzar, whiles he tasted the wine, commanded to bring the golden and silver vessels which his father Nebuchadnezzar had taken out of the temple which *was* in Jerusalem; that the king, and his princes, his wives, and his concubines, might drink therein. ³ Then they brought the golden vessels that were taken out of the temple of the house of God which *was* at Jerusalem; and the king, and his princes, his wives, and his concubines, drank in them. ⁴ They drank wine, and praised the gods of gold, and of silver, of brass, of iron, of wood, and of stone.

The King of Babylon gives a party for his lords, wives, concubines, princes, etc. in which he drinks to the point of drunkenness. He in his drunken stupor decides to mock the God of Israel by drinking from the vessels that his grandfather had taken from the temple in Jerusalem. This serves as an example of how strong drink makes a fool of a man.

- "¹ Wine *is* a mocker, strong drink *is* raging: and whosoever is deceived thereby is not wise." (Proverbs 20:1)
- "²⁹ Who hath woe? Who hath sorrow? Who hath contentions? Who hath babbling? Who hath wounds without cause? Who hath redness of eyes? ³⁰ They that tarry long at the wine; they that go to seek mixed wine. ³¹ Look not thou upon the wine when it is red, when it giveth his colour in the cup, *when* it moveth itself aright. ³² At the last it biteth like a serpent, and stingeth like an adder." (Proverbs 23:29-32)
- ¹¹ Woe unto them that rise up early in the morning, *that* they may follow strong drink; that continue until night, *till* wine inflame them! ¹² And the harp, and the viol, the tabret, and pipe, and wine, are in their feasts: but they regard not the work of the LORD, neither consider the operation of his hands. ¹³ Therefore my people are gone into captivity, because *they have* no knowledge: and their honourable men *are* famished, and their multitude dried up with thirst. ¹⁴ Therefore hell hath enlarged herself, and opened her mouth without measure: and their glory, and their multitude, and their pomp, and he that rejoiceth, shall descend into it. ¹⁵ And the mean man shall be brought down, and the mighty man shall be humbled, and the eyes of the lofty shall be humbled: ¹⁶ But the LORD of hosts shall be exalted in judgment, and God that is holy shall be sanctified in righteousness.(Isaiah 5:11-16)

The Writing on the Wall

Daniel 5:5-7

⁵ In the same hour came forth fingers of a man's hand, and wrote over against the candlestick upon the plaister of the wall of the king's palace: and the king saw the part of the hand that wrote. ⁶ Then the king's countenance was changed, and his thoughts troubled him, so that the joints of his loins were loosed, and his knees smote one against another. ⁷ The king cried aloud to bring in the astrologers, the Chaldeans, and the soothsayers. *And* the king spake, and said to the wise *men* of Babylon, Whosoever shall read this writing, and shew me the interpretation thereof, shall be clothed with scarlet, and *have* a chain of gold about his neck, and shall be the third ruler in the kingdom.

Belshazzar Mocks the God of Israel

All indication is that this feast is going on while the city is under siege by the Medes and the Persians. Belshazzar is feeling secure in his palace and begins to get drunk, drinking from the vessels taken from the house of the Lord. As he drank, a hand appears and begins to write on the wall of the palace. The king sobers up quickly. He calls for his wise men and searches for answers from the wisdom of this world. In Isaiah 47:7-15 the Lord tells us what He thinks of the wisdom of the Chaldeans (See also 1Cor. 2:6-12 on the wisdom of this world). Belshazzar offers to anyone who can interpret the dream the third in rulership in his kingdom. That would be after his dad and himself. Note that Belshazzar is actually Nebuchadnezzar's grandson. According to secular history, he actually reigned with his father. Jeremiah 27:6-7 says that Israel would be captive of Nebuchadnezzar, his son and his son's son.

Daniel 5:8-9

⁸ Then came in all the king's wise *men*: but they could not read the writing, nor make known to the king the interpretation thereof. ⁹ Then was king Belshazzar greatly troubled, and his countenance was changed in him, and his lords were astonied.

Here the king's wise men were faced with the word of God and could read it but could not understand it. This is the truth of 1Corinthians 2:10-14, that the natural man does not receive the deep things of the Spirit of God and can not understand the deep things of God.

Daniel 5:10-12

[10] *Now* the queen, by reason of the words of the king and his lords, came into the banquet house: *and* the queen spake and said, O king, live for ever: let not thy thoughts trouble thee, nor let thy countenance be changed: [11] There is a man in thy kingdom, in whom *is* the spirit of the holy gods; and in the days of thy father light and understanding and wisdom, like the wisdom of the gods, was found in him; whom the king Nebuchadnezzar thy father, the king, *I say*, thy father, made master of the magicians, astrologers, Chaldeans, *and* soothsayers; [12] Forasmuch as an excellent spirit, and knowledge, and understanding, interpreting of dreams, and shewing of hard sentences, and dissolving of doubts, were found in the same Daniel, whom the king named Belteshazzar: now let Daniel be called, and he will shew the interpretation.

The queen remembers the similar experience that his grandfather had about 60 years earlier. She introduces him to Daniel who his grandfather made head over the wise men.

Daniel 5:13-16

[13] Then was Daniel brought in before the king. *And* the king spake and said unto Daniel, *Art* thou that Daniel, which *art* of the children of the captivity of Judah, whom the king my father brought out of Jewry? [14] I have even heard of thee, that the spirit of the gods *is* in thee, and *that* light and understanding and excellent wisdom is found in thee. [15] And now the wise *men*, the astrologers, have been brought in before me, that they should read this writing, and make known unto me the interpretation thereof: but they could not shew the interpretation of the thing: [16] And I have heard of thee, that thou canst make interpretations, and dissolve doubts: now if thou canst read the writing, and make known to me the interpretation thereof, thou shalt be clothed with scarlet, and *have* a chain of gold about thy neck, and shalt be the third ruler in the kingdom.

Belshazzar recognizes the captivity of the Jews and probably suspects that the writing is connected with the desecration of the vessel of the temple. From his words in Verse 14 we see that he considers the God of Daniel as being just another of the many gods. He just does not get it, but he will soon learn of the true God.

Daniel 5:17-21

[17] Then Daniel answered and said before the king, Let thy gifts be to thyself, and give thy rewards to another; yet I will read the writing unto the king, and make known to him the interpretation. [18] O thou king, the most high God gave Nebuchadnezzar thy father a kingdom, and majesty, and glory, and honour: [19] And for the majesty that he gave him, all people, nations, and languages, trembled and feared before him: whom he would he slew; and whom he would he kept alive; and whom he would he set up; and whom he would he put down. [20] But when his heart was lifted up, and his mind hardened in pride, he was deposed from his kingly throne, and they took his glory from him: [21] And he was driven from the sons of men; and his heart was made like the beasts, and his dwelling *was* with the wild asses: they fed him with grass like oxen, and his body was wet with the dew of heaven;

till he knew that the most high God ruled in the kingdom of men, and *that* he appointeth over it whomsoever he will.

Daniel recounts the experience that Belshazzar's grandfather had some 15 years earlier. That experience taught Nebuchadnezzar to humble himself before the Most High God. Belshazzar knew this but would not humble himself.

Daniel 5:22 - 23

[22] And thou his son, O Belshazzar, hast not humbled thine heart, though thou knewest all this; [23] But hast lifted up thyself against the Lord of heaven; and they have brought the vessels of his house before thee, and thou, and thy lords, thy wives, and thy concubines, have drunk wine in them; and thou hast praised the gods of silver, and gold, of brass, iron, wood, and stone, which see not, nor hear, nor know: and the God in whose hand thy breath *is*, and whose *are* all thy ways, hast thou not glorified:

God's Indictment against Belshazzar

Daniel brings a four count indictment against Belshazzar -- though it is God's word that brings it. This must have taken courage to do so to the one who, at a word, could have him put to death. However, Daniel is more concerned about the Word of God than the hurt feelings of the king. The indictment:

1. He refused to give glory to God (vs. 21).
2. He rejected the counsel of God that he should have gotten from what happened to his grandfather (vs. 22).
3. He did not humble his heart as Nebuchadnezzar did.
4. He mocked God by drinking of the vessels from the temple (vs. 23) and attributed the glory that should be God's to idols.

Daniel 5:24-28

[24] Then was the part of the hand sent from him; and this writing was written. [25] And this *is* the writing that was written, MENE, MENE, TEKEL, UPHARSIN. [26] This *is* the interpretation of the thing: MENE; God hath numbered thy kingdom, and finished it. [27] TEKEL; Thou art weighed in the balances, and art found wanting. [28] PERES; Thy kingdom is divided, and given to the Medes and Persians.

The writing was from the hand of God (vs. 24). The interpretation is given:

*   MENE MENE – God had numbered the duration of the days of Belshazzar's kingdom and his number is up.
*   TEKEL – Belshazzar was weighted in the balance and did not measure up.
*   PERES – His kingdom was given to the Medes and Persians who were laying siege to the city at that moment.

Daniel 5:29-30

[29] Then commanded Belshazzar, and they clothed Daniel with scarlet, and *put* a chain of gold about his neck, and made a proclamation concerning him, that he should be the third ruler in the kingdom. [30] In that night was Belshazzar the king of the Chaldeans slain.

From all appearance, Belshazzar was not moved by the interpretation or the indictment. Such is the hardness that pride (the pride that accompanies unbelief) that a stubborn rejection of truth puts into the heart. He gives Daniel the gift that he promised (which Daniel had no interest in – Verse 17) and retires for the night.

Daniel 5:31

³¹ And Darius the Median took the kingdom, *being* about threescore and two years old.

That night, Darius the Mede takes the kingdom. Cyrus the Persian eventually succeeded him. Cyrus (Ezra 1:1-4) was named in the Bible about 170 years before he came to the throne (Isa. 44:28). Though Isaiah prophesies of the fall of Babylon, the city will again be rebuilt and will suffer another great fall in the Tribulation period – a fall from which it will never recover (Rev. 14:8).

The biblical order of the monarchs of Daniel's time, and of the period of the captivity and restoration of Judah, is as follows:

(1) Nebuchadnezzar (B.C. 604-561) with whom the captivity of Judah and the "times of the Gentiles" began, and who established the first of the four world monarchies.

(2) Belshazzar (probably B.C. 556), the Bel-shar-uzzar of the inscriptions, grandson of Nebuchadnezzar, and son of the victorious general Nabonidus is the second. Belshazzar seems to have reigned as viceroy under Nabonidus.

(3) Darius the Mede took the kingdom at the age of 62. (Daniel 5:31). We see him throughout chapter 6 though he ruled for only two years. We see him again mentioned in Daniel 9:1. There seems to be little mention of him outside of this book of Daniel. He has been conjectured to be identical with Gobryas, a Persian general. This Darius was "the son of Ahasuerus, of the seed of the Medes, which was made king over the realm of the Chaldeans" (Dan. 9:1) "Ahasuerus," more a title than a name, the equivalent of the modern "Majesty," is used in Scripture of at least four personages, and is Persian rather than Median. That Darius the Mede was the "son" (or grandson) of an Ahasuerus proves no more than that he was, probably, through the seed of his mother, of the seed royal not only of Media, but also of Persia. There is but one Darius in Daniel

(4) Cyrus (the son of Darius' sister Mundane and of Cambyses) whose rise to power brought fully into existence the Medo-Persian kingdom -- second of the world-empires (Dan. 2:39, 7:5). In Daniel's vision of this empire in "the third year of the reign of King Belshazzar" (Dan. 8:1-4), the Median power of Darius is seen as the lesser of the two horns of the ram. The Persian power of Cyrus, under whom the Medo-Persian power was consolidated, was the "higher" horn which "came up last." It was under Cyrus, who was prophetically named more than a century before his birth (Isa. 44:28; 45:1-4) that the return of the Jewish remnant to Palestine began (Ezra 1:1-4.

Daniel Chapter 5: Study Guide Questions

1. What is Belshazzar's relationship to Nebuchadnezzar?

2. In Verse 31, we see that Darius the Mede conquered the city of Babylon the night after this drunken party was over. What does that say about where Darius was during this party?

3. Does Belshazzar feel secure in his palace while this party was going on? What was he putting his trust in for his security? How sure was that security in the end? Can there be any true security for anyone who is mocking God?

4. What was the important lesson that Nebuchadnezzar learned but which he failed to teach to his son and his son's son? Does this teach us something about what we should teach our children and our children's children?

5. What was the four count indictment that Daniel issued against Belshazzar?

6. What was the three part message that God gives to Belshazzar?

7. What country was Darius from? What country was Cyrus from?

Chapter 6
Daniel under the Medes and Persians

Daniel 6:1-3 (KJV)

> [1] It pleased Darius to set over the kingdom an hundred and twenty princes, which should be over the whole kingdom; [2] And over these three presidents; of whom Daniel *was* first: that the princes might give accounts unto them, and the king should have no damage. [3] Then this Daniel was preferred above the presidents and princes, because an excellent spirit *was* in him; and the king thought to set him over the whole realm.

Here in Chapter 6 we move on in history to the second in the sequence of the kingdoms we saw mentioned in Daniel Chapter 2 in the great image. We are now in the Medio-Persian phase of the times of the Gentiles and find Daniel is still the prime minister. Darius sets 120 princes over the kingdom. Over these 120 he set three presidents of which Daniel was the first. Darius preferred Daniel over all of them because of an excellent spirit that he saw in Daniel. That excellent spirit ought to be in every believer. The world should be able to look at a believer and see that there is something different about him when compared with the unbelievers around him.

So who is Darius? "Darius is the Darius Cyaxares II of secular history, and he ruled for only two years. Cyrus, who followed him, was the son of Darius' sister Mundane and of Cambyses the Persians. This was what brought the empire together into the Medo-Persian Empire which now ruled the world." (Thru The Bible with J. Vernon McGee.)

Daniel 6:4-5

> [4] Then the presidents and princes sought to find occasion against Daniel concerning the kingdom; but they could find none occasion nor fault; forasmuch as he *was* faithful, neither was there any error or fault found in him. [5] Then said these men, We shall not find any occasion against this Daniel, except we find *it* against him concerning the law of his God.

These princes of the kingdom are moved with jealousy to try to find fault with Daniel, but are unable to because of his faithfulness. There was neither error nor fault to be found in Daniel. What a testimony of faithfulness he should be for us. People like to work with people that they can trust. As believers, we must always be trustworthy.

They realize that the only way that they can find occasion to condemn him is to find fault with his God. This is the same situation that the Scribes and Pharisees were in when confronted with the truth of the Lord.

John 8:38-50

> "[38] I speak that which I have seen with my Father: and ye do that which ye have seen with your father. [39] They answered and said unto him, Abraham is our father. Jesus saith unto them, If ye were Abraham's children, ye would do the works of Abraham. [40] But now ye seek to kill me, a man that hath told you the truth, which I have heard of God: this did not Abraham. [41] Ye do the deeds of your father. Then said they to him, We be not born of fornication; we have one Father, *even* God. [42]

Jesus said unto them, If God were your Father, ye would love me: for I proceeded forth and came from God; neither came I of myself, but he sent me. [43] Why do ye not understand my speech? *Even* because ye cannot hear my word. [44] Ye are of *your* father the devil, and the lusts of your father ye will do. He was a murderer from the beginning, and abode not in the truth, because there is no truth in him. When he speaketh a lie, he speaketh of his own: for he is a liar, and the father of it. [45] And because I tell *you* the truth, ye believe me not. [46] Which of you convinceth me of sin? And if I say the truth, why do ye not believe me? [47] He that is of God heareth God's words: ye therefore hear *them* not, because ye are not of God. [48] Then answered the Jews, and said unto him, Say we not well that thou art a Samaritan, and hast a devil? (John 8:38-50) [49] Jesus answered, I have not a devil; but I honour my Father, and ye do dishonour me. [50] And I seek not mine own glory: there is one that seeketh and judgeth." (John 8:38-50)

Since they can not find fault with Daniel they conspire to find fault with him by means of a false religious system. Here again he is a type of Christ. The Scribes and Pharisees sought occasion against the Lord not in the Law of Moses but in the commandments of men as the Lord tells them in Mark 7:8 "…laying aside the commandment of God, ye hold the tradition of men…"

Daniel 6:6-9

[6] Then these presidents and princes assembled together to the king, and said thus unto him, King Darius, live for ever. [7] All the presidents of the kingdom, the governors, and the princes, the counselors, and the captains, have consulted together to establish a royal statute, and to make a firm decree, that whosoever shall ask a petition of any God or man for thirty days, save of thee, O king, he shall be cast into the den of lions. [8] Now, O king, establish the decree, and sign the writing, that it be not changed, according to the law of the Medes and Persians, which altereth not. [9] Wherefore king Darius signed the writing and the decree.

They come up with a plan to establish a "state religion" that contradicts the true religion of Jewry. This is a good study in why it is not a good idea to have a state religion. What state is there that, if it were to establish a religion, would not establish it on false doctrine? How important it is therefore that we understand that in the inspired and preserved Word of God we have the final authority in all matters of faith and practice. The king is ignorant of the scheming of the jealous princes and becomes an unwitting accomplice in the scheme.

Daniel 6:10

[10] Now when Daniel knew that the writing was signed, he went into his house; and his windows being open in his chamber toward Jerusalem, he kneeled upon his knees three times a day, and prayed, and gave thanks before his God, as he did aforetime.

Here Daniel does what Israel is instructed to do when they can not gain access to the temple service to make a sacrifice because of their captivity – they are to pray toward the holy city (1Kings 8:44-49; Psalm 5:7; Jonah 2:4). Therefore, Daniel prays as he is instructed even though he knows of the decree of the king. Daniel understood that he had another option to live up to the requirements of the law (Psalm 141:1 & 2).

He understands that the commandments of God override the commandments of men. We take instruction from this to always do what is right (Acts 5:29; Jer. 11:3).

Daniel 6:11-13

[11] Then these men assembled, and found Daniel praying and making supplication before his God. [12] Then they came near, and spake before the king concerning the king's decree; Hast thou not signed a decree, that every man that shall ask *a petition* of any God or man within thirty days, save of thee, O king, shall be cast into the den of lions? The king answered and said, The thing *is* true, according to the law of the Medes and Persians, which altereth not. [13] Then answered they and said before the king, That Daniel, which *is* of the children of the captivity of Judah, regardeth not thee, O king, nor the decree that thou hast signed, but maketh his petition three times a day.

The jealous princes tell the king of Daniel's disobedience to the king's command. They then point out that the king has no choice but to send Daniel to the lion's den.

Daniel 6:14-15

[14] Then the king, when he heard *these* words, was sore displeased with himself, and set *his* heart on Daniel to deliver him: and he laboured till the going down of the sun to deliver him. [15] Then these men assembled unto the king, and said unto the king, Know, O king, that the law of the Medes and Persians *is*, That no decree nor statute which the king establisheth may be changed.

Darius labored until the last minute to find a way to release Daniel. This is a type of the situation that God the Father found Himself in with regard to justifying sinners and His desire to save His only begotten Son who was to go to the cross in order to redeem man. Here Darius who loved Daniel could not violate his own system of justice to save him from the lion's den. Regarding Calvary, the Father out of a heart of love for the lost desired that he might justify sinners. However, his holiness demanded that He be separate from sin and also his justice demanded that sin be punished. He (Jesus who knew no sin) was made to be sin for us (who did the sinning), that we might be made the righteousness of God in Him (2Cor. 5:21; Rom. 3:25-26)

Daniel 6:16-18

[16] Then the king commanded, and they brought Daniel, and cast *him* into the den of lions. *Now* the king spake and said unto Daniel, Thy God whom thou servest continually, he will deliver thee. [17] And a stone was brought, and laid upon the mouth of the den; and the king sealed it with his own signet, and with the signet of his lords; that the purpose might not be changed concerning Daniel. [18] Then the king went to his palace, and passed the night fasting: neither were instruments of musick brought before him: and his sleep went from him.

Here the justice for the king's broken commandment has to be satisfied. This again is a type of Calvary. The justice of the broken law had to be satisfied. The king passes the night in fasting and prayer without sleep for the deliverance of Daniel.

Daniel 6:19-22

¹⁹ Then the king arose very early in the morning, and went in haste unto the den of lions. ²⁰ And when he came to the den, he cried with a lamentable voice unto Daniel: *and* the king spake and said to Daniel, O Daniel, servant of the living God, is thy God, whom thou servest continually, able to deliver thee from the lions? ²¹ Then said Daniel unto the king, O king, live for ever. ²² My God hath sent his angel, and hath shut the lions' mouths, that they have not hurt me: forasmuch as before him innocency was found in me; and also before thee, O king, have I done no hurt.

The king is grieved with what he had to do. We notice that his attitude has changed. In his hour a deepest need, he reaches out to the true God in faith for deliverance for Daniel. Note the evidence of true conversion in his plea: "O Daniel, servant of the living God…" (Verse 20) Here Daniel's faithfulness led to the conversion of the Gentile king. This is what Israel was to do in the world but failed because of their lack of faithfulness. Daniel had been faithful to the king (Eph 6:5; Col 3:22). That is a lesson for us to note today "¹⁷ For our light affliction, which is but for a moment, worketh for us a far more exceeding *and* eternal weight of glory; ¹⁸ While we look not at the things which are seen, but at the things which are not seen: for the things which are seen *are* temporal; but the things which are not seen *are* eternal." (2Cor.4:17-18). Faithfulness for us is much like Abraham's faith whereby he "when he was called to go out into a place which he should after receive for an inheritance, obeyed; and he went out, not knowing whither he went." (Heb. 11:8)

Daniel 6:23-24

²³ Then was the king exceeding glad for him, and commanded that they should take Daniel up out of the den. So Daniel was taken up out of the den, and no manner of hurt was found upon him, because he believed in his God. ²⁴ And the king commanded, and they brought those men which had accused Daniel, and they cast *them* into the den of lions, them, their children, and their wives; and the lions had the mastery of them, and brake all their bones in pieces or ever they came at the bottom of the den.

Daniel was delivered because he believed in God. His wicked and deceitful accusers however suffered the fate that they would have seen imposed upon Daniel. This is a lesson in sowing and reaping. It is what we call the law of the harvest (Gal. 5:7-8): We reap what we sow, we reap after we sow, and we reap more than we sow.

Daniel 6:25-27

²⁵ Then king Darius wrote unto all people, nations, and languages, that dwell in all the earth; Peace be multiplied unto you. ²⁶ I make a decree, That in every dominion of my kingdom men tremble and fear before the God of Daniel: for he *is* the living God, and stedfast for ever, and his kingdom *that* which shall not be destroyed, and his dominion *shall be even* unto the end. ²⁷ He delivereth and rescueth, and he worketh signs and wonders in heaven and in earth, who hath delivered Daniel from the power of the lions.

Faithfulness of believers always brings praise to God. How important it is that we always remember that when we face temptation to compromise the Word of God to not take the easy way out.

Daniel 6:28

^{28} So this Daniel prospered in the reign of Darius, and in the reign of Cyrus the Persian.

Darius the Mede and Cyrus the Persian are two Gentile kings who were converted to God by Daniel's faithfulness. The effect that his life had on these two kings is the effect that Israel as a nation was to have on all that were around them. This too is an important lesson for us as the fate of men around us is dependent upon our faithfulness to live according to the Word to us – the Word rightly divided. For us that lessen is to live according to the preaching of Jesus Christ according to the revelation of the mystery which was kept hid in God until He revealed it to and through the apostle Paul.

Daniel Chapter 6: Study Guide Questions

1. What did Darius see in Daniel that prompted him to put Daniel in position as the first president in his cabinet?

2. What was the heart attitude of the 120 princes towards Daniel?

3. What was the only thing that the princes could turn to in order to find occasion against Daniel?

4. What fault was there in Darius that opened him up to the deception that allowed the princes to set both the king and Daniel up in a trap?

5. Did Daniel compromise any as a result of the apparent trap?

6. What similitude do you see between Darius and Daniel in this ordeal and that of God the Father and Jesus regarding Calvary?

7. What evidence do you see in verse 20 that there was a genuine conversion of Darius to the true God?

8. Do you see God using this incident to open the door for the gospel of the true God to go into the Gentile world? Was Israel the instrumental means of this outreach or was God doing this in spite of Israel's failure to reach out to the Gentiles?

Daniel Chapter 7
The Beast Visions of Daniel

Daniel 7:1 (KJV)

[1] In the first year of Belshazzar king of Babylon Daniel had a dream and visions of his head upon his bed: then he wrote the dream, *and* told the sum of the matters.

Prior to Daniel chapter 7, Daniel (in the book of Daniel) interprets the dreams of others. Now he starts to present dreams that he had himself dreamed. The focus from here on is on those dreams that he personally had.

Daniel 7: 2-3

[2] Daniel spake and said, I saw in my vision by night, and, behold, the four winds of the heaven strove upon the great sea. [3] And four great beasts came up from the sea, diverse one from another.

Daniel refers to the "…vision by night…" and "…the night vision…" often in these dreams. The term "night" is significant in prophecy as is the word "day". The "day" in prophecy is the day of the Lord when the Lord receives what is rightfully His. The "night" then is the rest of the time when Christ is absent from the earth while the earth is under the control of "the god of this world" (Eph. 2:2). In John 8:12 the Lord reveals Himself as the light of the world: "[12] Then spake Jesus again unto them, saying, I am the light of the world: he that followeth me shall not walk in darkness, but shall have the light of life."

Paul tells us that we are of the day. The night will end when the Lord returns to the earth.

"[1] But of the times and the seasons, brethren, ye have no need that I write unto you. [2] For yourselves know perfectly that the day of the Lord so cometh as a thief in the night. [3] For when they shall say, Peace and safety; then sudden destruction cometh upon them, as travail upon a woman with child; and they shall not escape. [4] But ye, brethren, are not in darkness, that that day should overtake you as a thief. [5] Ye are all the children of light, and the children of the day: we are not of the night, nor of darkness." (1Thess 5:1-5)

Paul tells the Romans that the night (the times when the Gentiles rule this world) is far spent and that the day is at hand. The day for us is when the Lord comes for His church to catch it away to heaven. It is then that our salvation will be complete. "[11] And that, knowing the time, that now *it is* high time to awake out of sleep: for now *is* our salvation nearer than when we believed. [12] The night is far spent, the day is at hand: let us therefore cast off the works of darkness, and let us put on the armour of light. [13] Let us walk honestly, as in the day; not in rioting and drunkenness, not in chambering and wantonness, not in strife and envying." (Romans 13:11-13)

The night of Bible prophecy began when Israel was taken captive. The captivity was prophesied in Deuteronomy 28:28, 49-52, and 63-66. In 2Kings 18:9ff we see the account of the Lord delivering Judah from captivity by Assyria even though Israel (the ten northern tribes) were taken captive. The night began in 2Chronicles 36:1-21 when Nebuchadnezzar took Jehoiakim captive to Babylon. In 2Kings, the siege that resulted in Judah being taken captive began in the 9th year of the reign of Zedekiah in the 10th month in the

10th day. Daniel 2:29-45 describes the sequence of the nations that held Israel captive. The times of the Gentiles will actually end with the battle of Armageddon (Rev. 16:19; Luke 21:24).

In Daniel's dream, the four winds of heaven strove on the great sea. This is likely a reference to the Mediterranean Sea. Daniel sees four great beasts come up out of the sea – that would be countries in the Mediterranean area. We will see that there are four kings (Verse 17) and four kingdoms that arise in succession in that area.

Daniel 7:4

> ⁴ The first *was* like a lion, and had eagle's wings: I beheld till the wings thereof were plucked, and it was lifted up from the earth, and made stand upon the feet as a man, and a man's heart was given to it.

This first beast was like a lion and had eagle's wings. Jeremiah the prophet speaks of the coming Babylonian captivity in Jeremiah 4:7 using the figurative language of a lion: "⁷ The lion is come up from his thicket, and the destroyer of the Gentiles is on his way; he is gone forth from his place to make thy land desolate; *and* thy cities shall be laid waste, without an inhabitant." Again in Jeremiah 25:9 we see the 70 years of captivity starting with the capture of the city by Babylon: "⁸ Therefore thus saith the LORD of hosts; Because ye have not heard my words, ⁹ Behold, I will send and take all the families of the north, saith the LORD, and Nebuchadnezzar the king of Babylon, my servant, and will bring them against this land, and against the inhabitants thereof, and against all these nations round about, and will utterly destroy them, and make them an astonishment, and an hissing, and perpetual desolations."

In Ezekiel 17:3-5 we find a riddle that is at first difficult to figure out. The riddle uses the figure of a great eagle that carried Jerusalem away captive: "³ And say, Thus saith the Lord GOD; A great eagle with great wings, longwinged, full of feathers, which had divers colours, came unto Lebanon, and took the highest branch of the cedar: ⁴ He cropped off the top of his young twigs, and carried it into a land of traffick; he set it in a city of merchants. ⁵ He took also of the seed of the land, and planted it in a fruitful field; he placed *it* by great waters, *and* set it *as* a willow tree." Then in Ezekiel 17:12 we see that the great eagle is identified as the king of Babylon. The reference to Lebanon is likely a reference to conquest of Assyria. Babylon conquered Egypt and Syria before conquering Israel.

Daniel 7:5

> ⁵ And behold another beast, a second, like to a bear, and it raised up itself on one side, and *it had* three ribs in the mouth of it between the teeth of it: and they said thus unto it, Arise, devour much flesh.

Here a second beast succeeds the first. This one is like a bear. It raised itself up on one side and had three ribs between its teeth. If this be the third kingdom, then the ribs would be Babylon, Media, and Persia. We consider who the "they" are that says "arise, devour much flesh." The book of Daniel focuses on the angels as watchers (angels) in the affairs of men and even as intermediaries (Dan. 4:17; 10:13, 14, 20, and 33). The wind in Verse 2 is a type of the spirit world (John 3:8). The prophetic events in the affairs of men are influenced by the spirit world (2Kings 6:17). The fact remains that "The heavens do rule" (Dan. 4:12, 26). Even today, the spirit world influences life on earth (Eph. 2:2; 2Cor. 4:4).

Daniel 7:6

⁶ After this I beheld, and lo another, like a leopard, which had upon the back of it four wings of a fowl; the beast had also four heads; and dominion was given to it.

Here we see a third beast that is like a leopard. It has four wings upon its back. This would be Alexander the Great with the four wings and the four heads representing the four generals in his conquering army who divided his kingdom among themselves after his death (Dan. 8:22).

Daniel 7:7-8

⁷ After this I saw in the night visions, and behold a fourth beast, dreadful and terrible, and strong exceedingly; and it had great iron teeth: it devoured and brake in pieces, and stamped the residue with the feet of it: and it *was* diverse from all the beasts that *were* before it; and it had ten horns. ⁸ I considered the horns, and, behold, there came up among them another little horn, before whom there were three of the first horns plucked up by the roots: and, behold, in this horn *were* eyes like the eyes of man, and a mouth speaking great things.

This fourth beast is apparently the antichrist. Note here again it is in the "night vision." This beast is more note-worthy than the others that preceded it in that it is diverse from the others. It is dreadful and terrible and strong exceedingly. It has great iron teeth. Iron is associated with demonic intermixing with men (Dan. 2:43). It has ten horns. A horn in Bible prophecy represents a kingdom (Rev. 17:8-16). Another horn comes up among them. The horn that comes up last is the antichrist. The antichrist starts out with a confederacy of 10 kings (Psalm 83). He conquers three of them (Revelation 17:12). The others capitulate and give him their power and authority. The last horn had eyes and a mouth speaking great things. The eyes represent the "ll seeing eye" that tracks the activity of men for the purpose of gaining control of man. We today have it on the dollar bill. The great things that the mouth speaks are blasphemy against God as we see in 2Thessalonians 2:4).

The little horn of Verse 8 is the one who is called the antichrist. There are many names given to him in the Bible. He is:

- the "king of fierce countenance" (Daniel 8:23-25)
- the "prince that shall come" of Daniel 9:26,27
- the "king" of Daniel 11:36-45
- the "abomination" of Daniel 12:11 and Matthew 12:11
- the "man of sin" of 2Thessalonians 2:4-8
- and the "Beast" of Revelation 13:4-10 See Schofield's note on "Beast" in Daniel 7:8 and Revelation 19:20

Daniel 7:9-10

⁹ I beheld till the thrones were cast down, and the Ancient of days did sit, whose garment *was* white as snow, and the hair of his head like the pure wool: his throne *was like* the fiery flame, *and* his wheels *as* burning fire. ¹⁰ A fiery stream issued and came forth from before him: thousand thousands ministered unto him, and ten thousand times ten thousand stood before him: the judgment was set, and the books were opened.

The thrones of the four beasts were cast down when the Ancient of Days did sit on his throne. 1,000,000 ministered to Him and 100,000,000 stood before Him. This is God the Father reigning in the person of His Son (cf. Verse 13) Christ at the judgment of the nations. The books were opened. This takes us to Revelation 20:12 where we see this fulfilled at the great white throne. Malachi 3:16-18 speaks of a book of remembrance.

Daniel 7:11

¹¹ I beheld then because of the voice of the great words which the horn spake: I beheld *even* till the beast was slain, and his body destroyed, and given to the burning flame.

This verse looks forward to the time that the antichrist is cast into the lake of fire which finally happens in Revelation 19:20.

Daniel 7:12

¹² As concerning the rest of the beasts, they had their dominion taken away: yet their lives were prolonged for a season and time.

This is interesting! They have their dominion taken away, but their lives are prolonged for a season and a time. The four beasts go through time and appear in time at different times but they are all there again together during the last days. These four kingdoms succeed each other in reigning over Israel but they are again players in the end time events.

Daniel 7:13-14

¹³ I saw in the night visions, and, behold, *one* like the Son of man came with the clouds of heaven, and came to the Ancient of days, and they brought him near before him. ¹⁴ And there was given him dominion, and glory, and a kingdom, that all people, nations, and languages, should serve him: his dominion *is* an everlasting dominion, which shall not pass away, and his kingdom *that* which shall not be destroyed.

Here we see Christ receiving the Kingdom from the Father (Rev. 5:1-8). The clouds are angels (Luke 19:10; Matt. 8:20; Rev. 14:14).

Daniel 7:15-18

¹⁵ I Daniel was grieved in my spirit in the midst of *my* body, and the visions of my head troubled me. ¹⁶ I came near unto one of them that stood by, and asked him the truth of all this. So he told me, and made me know the interpretation of the things. ¹⁷ These great beasts, which are four, *are* four kings, *which* shall arise out of the earth. ¹⁸ But the saints of the most High shall take the kingdom, and possess the kingdom for ever, even for ever and ever.

Daniel approaches one of the angels that stand by to seek to understand the dream. The angel interprets the dream saying that the four beasts are four kings that <u>shall</u> arise out of the earth. It should be noted here that Babylon and Persia are already past history as kingdoms when this was revealed. Therefore, we understand that these kings are yet future from where Daniel is at in time at the writing of the book of Daniel. There is obviously a near and far fulfillment of the prophecy. Ultimately however, it will be the saints of God who will possess the kingdom.

Daniel 7: 19-22

[19] Then I would know the truth of the fourth beast, which was diverse from all the others, exceeding dreadful, whose teeth *were of* iron, and his nails *of* brass; *which* devoured, brake in pieces, and stamped the residue with his feet; [20] And of the ten horns that *were* in his head, and *of* the other which came up, and before whom three fell; even *of* that horn that had eyes, and a mouth that spake very great things, whose look *was* more stout than his fellows. [21] I beheld, and the same horn made war with the saints, and prevailed against them; [22] Until the Ancient of days came, and judgment was given to the saints of the most High; and the time came that the saints possessed the kingdom.

Daniel's curiosity is drawn to the fourth beast and he inquires further of the angel. Note the Ancient of Days is God the Father in the person of His Son Jesus.

Daniel 7:23

[23] Thus he said, The fourth beast shall be the fourth kingdom upon earth, which shall be diverse from all kingdoms, and shall devour the whole earth, and shall tread it down, and break it in pieces.

The fourth beast is the fourth kingdom after Babylon, Media-Persia, and Greece. This king shall be different than those that came before. He will devour, tread down and break in pieces the whole earth. This would be the kingdom of the antichrist. Though the antichrist's kingdom extends only over ten nations, his influence extends over the entire earth.

Daniel 7:24

[24] And the ten horns out of this kingdom *are* ten kings *that* shall arise: and another shall rise after them; and he shall be diverse from the first, and he shall subdue three kings.

The antichrist's kingdom extends only over these ten kings. He conquers three of them and the other seven capitulate to him.

Daniel 7:25

[25] And he shall speak *great* words against the most High, and shall wear out the saints of the most High, and think to change times and laws: and they shall be given into his hand until a time and times and the dividing of time.

This time and times and the dividing of time is the second half of the tribulation period that we see in Revelation 12:14. The great things that he speaks against the Most High are referred to in 2Thessalonians 2:3-4 "[3] Let no man deceive you by any means: for *that day shall not come*, except there come a falling away first, and that man of sin be revealed, the son of perdition; [4] Who opposeth and exalteth himself above all that is called God, or that is worshipped; so that he as God sitteth in the temple of God, shewing himself that he is God."

Daniel 7:26-27

> [26] But the judgment shall sit, and they shall take away his dominion, to consume and to destroy *it* unto the end. [27] And the kingdom and dominion, and the greatness of the kingdom under the whole heaven, shall be given to the people of the saints of the Most High, whose kingdom *is* an everlasting kingdom, and all dominions shall serve and obey him.

The fourth beast is taken in Revelation 19:19-20. "[19] And I saw the beast, and the kings of the earth, and their armies, gathered together to make war against him that sat on the horse, and against his army. [20] And the beast was taken, and with him the false prophet that wrought miracles before him, with which he deceived them that had received the mark of the beast, and them that worshipped his image. These both were cast alive into a lake of fire burning with brimstone."

The "People of the Saints of the Most High God" in Verse 27 is a reference to the nation of Israel.

Daniel 7:28

> [28] Hitherto *is* the end of the matter. As for me Daniel, my cogitations much troubled me, and my countenance changed in me: but I kept the matter in my heart.

The prophecy changed Daniel. The blessing of knowing the truth of the word of God rightly divided will also change us.

Daniel Chapter 7: Study Guide Questions

1. How does the interpreting of dreams change starting in Chapter 7? What is significant about these dreams being referred to as "vision by night"? What is the difference between "Day" and "Night" in Bible prophecy?

2. When did the "Night" of Bible Prophecy begin? When will it end?

3. What was the sequence of nations that hold Israel captive? Give the passage in Daniel that lists them.

4. What event will end the "Times of the Gentiles?"

5. What "sea" would Verse 3 be referring to?

6. Identify the beast of verse 4.

7. Why is Nebuchadnezzar referred to as God's servant in Jeremiah 25:9?

8. Who does the great eagle in Verse 4 refer to? Compare this with Ezekiel 17 to find the answer.

9. Identify the beast of Verse 5. Who are the "they" of verse 5?

10. Who does the beast of verse 6 represent? Why are there four wings?

11. How is the fourth beast of verses 7-8 different from the three that went before?

12. Who is the "Ancient of Days" in Verse 9?

13. Verse 12 suggests that the lives of these beasts were prolonged. What does this suggest about the time of their tenure of earth?

14. Identify: 1) The Son of Man, 2) the clouds of heaven, and 3) the Ancient of Days in Verse 17. Are these four kings in Verse 17 in past history or are they in future prophecy?

15. What is the significance of the ten horns and the little horn that comes up later?

16. What is the extent of the influence of the fourth beast according to Verse 23? What will be the extent of his actual kingdom?

17. What is the "time and times, and the dividing of times" in Verse 25 referring to?

18. Who is the "Most High" of Verse 25? Who are the saints of the most high in Verse 26? Who are the people of the saints of the most high?

19.

Chapter 8
The Ram and the Rough Goat Vision

Daniel 8:1-4 (KJV)

[1] In the third year of the reign of king Belshazzar a vision appeared unto me, *even unto* me Daniel, after that which appeared unto me at the first. [2] And I saw in a vision; and it came to pass, when I saw, that I *was* at Shushan *in* the palace, which *is* in the province of Elam; and I saw in a vision, and I was by the river of Ulai. [3] Then I lifted up mine eyes, and saw, and, behold, there stood before the river a ram which had *two* horns: and the *two* horns *were* high; but one *was* higher than the other, and the higher came up last. [4] I saw the ram pushing westward, and northward, and southward; so that no beasts might stand before him, neither *was there any* that could deliver out of his hand; but he did according to his will, and became great.

We note here that that the section of the book of Daniel from Chapter 2 verse 4 to Chapter 7 verse 28 was written in Aramaic, the original language of Syria and the world language of these four great empires. Beginning here in Chapter 8, the book returns to the use of the Hebrew language.

The river Ulai is the river which flowed past the city Susa. Elam is the province in Persia in which Susa, the capital of the Persian Empire was located. Shusan was the palace of the royal family of the Persian monarchs. The Tigris River was on the western border of Elam. Daniel was apparently headquartered in Shushan during the reign of the Persian Empire.

The ram is the Medio-Persian Empire. (verse 20 cf. 7:5). The higher horn was Persian – the larger of the two kingdoms. These two kingdoms were joined (confederate) by marriage among the royal families. The ram pushed to the west, north and south. To the east was India and China. Persia never moved into the orient. No beast (i.e. Gentile kingdom) could stand against Persia in its day of power.

The He Goat

Daniel 8:5-8

[5] And as I was considering, behold, an he goat came from the west on the face of the whole earth, and touched not the ground: and the goat *had* a notable horn between his eyes. [6] And he came to the ram that had *two* horns, which I had seen standing before the river, and ran unto him in the fury of his power. [7] And I saw him come close unto the ram, and he was moved with choler against him, and smote the ram, and brake his two horns: and there was no power in the ram to stand before him, but he cast him down to the ground, and stamped upon him: and there was none that could deliver the ram out of his hand. [8] Therefore the he goat waxed very great: and when he was strong, the great horn was broken; and for it came up four notable ones toward the four winds of heaven.

The he goat is Greece (vs. 21 cf Dan 2:32, 39). The notable horn was Alexander the Great. (Dan. 11:3). When he was strong, the notable horn was broken. It is said by historians that after conquering the known world, Alexander wept because there were no more worlds to conquer. He died in Babylon in 323 BC at the age of 32 after a night long drinking party. After his death, his kingdom was divided up between his four generals as represented by the four heads of Daniel 7:6. The fourfold division was as follows:

- Casander (married to Alexander's sister) took Europe (Macedonia and Greece).
- Lysimachus took Asia Minor (Modern day Turkey).
- Seleucus took Asia – the eastern part of the empire except Egypt.
- Ptolomy took Egypt and north Africa.

The Little Horn

Daniel 8: 9-12

[9] And out of one of them came forth a little horn, which waxed exceeding great, toward the south, and toward the east, and toward the pleasant *land*. [10] And it waxed great, *even* to the host of heaven; and it cast down *some* of the host and of the stars to the ground, and stamped upon them. [11] Yea, he magnified *himself* even to the prince of the host, and by him the daily *sacrifice* was taken away, and the place of his sanctuary was cast down. [12] And an host was given *him* against the daily *sacrifice* by reason of transgression, and it cast down the truth to the ground; and it practiced, and prospered.

The little horn of verse 9 is the antichrist (Rev. 13:5, 7, 15, 17). The pleasant land is Israel (Ezek. 29:6, 15; Dan. 11:16; Zech. 7:14). The antichrist comes out of one of the divisions of the Greek empire. The question is: "Which one?" We will see more information later regarding this. This little horn is the beast out of the sea in Revelation 13. That beast (in Rev. 13) has seven heads and ten horns. The beast of Revelation 13 speaks "great things and blasphemies" for 42 months. He blasphemes God, God's name, and God's tabernacle and them that dwell in heaven (Rev. 13:5). At the time of the fulfillment of Revelation 13:5, the only dwellers in heaven will be God and His elect (both angelic and human). Satan will have been expelled from heaven by then (Rev. 12: 7-10). The little horn cast down some of the host and some of the stars to the ground. We see in Revelation 12:4 that the great red dragon which also has seven heads and ten horns "drew one third of the stars of heaven and did cast them to the earth." After he drew the hosts of heaven to the ground he stamped upon them. This is a gesture of taking over the domain of the defeated parties. We see this in verse 7 of Daniel 8 where the he goat (Alexander the Great) stamped upon the ram with the two horns. We understand from this that Satan defeated these hosts of heaven (Isa. 14:13). The stamping of the feet is symbolic of the total subjugating of the vanquished. We understand the little horn in relation to the other ten horns from Daniel 7:7-8. The little horn is the antichrist that rises to power after the ten horns (or the ten kings that the ten horns represent) rise to power. The little horn defeats three of the kings and the other seven capitulate and give him their power.

The little horn magnified himself even to the prince of the host. The prince of the host of heaven is the Lord Jesus Christ. It is by Jesus Christ that everything in heaven and in earth was created (Col. 1:12 and 13; John 4:1-4; Heb. 2:10). Joshua met Him as the captain of the host of the LORD (Josh. 5:14). The little horn magnified himself to the prince of the host just as Belshazzer did (Dan. 5:22 & 23) and lost his life and his kingdom for it. We saw the little horn speaking great words against the most high in Daniel 7:25.

In verse 11 we see that the little horn (the antichrist) takes away the daily sacrifice. Israel's sacrificial system will be reinstituted by the antichrist as a result of a covenant between him and the unbelieving nation of Israel. We will see this covenant between the antichrist and the unbelieving nation in Daniel 9:26. The Lord refers to that covenant as a covenant with death in Isaiah 28:15-18. The believing remnant of Israel will be telling the nation not to partake of that sacrificial system because they (the believing remnant) will be proclaiming the doctrine of the Book of Hebrews – i.e. "Neither by the blood of goats and calves, but by his own blood he entered in once into the holy place, having obtained eternal redemption for us. (Heb. 9:17; 10:19)

The place of the Lord's sanctuary is Jerusalem. Luke 21:20-28 speaks of the time during the tribulation period in the seventieth week of Daniel Chapter 9 that the antichrist will cast down Jerusalem in an attempt to foil God's plan for the city.

Daniel 8:13-14

¹³ Then I heard one saint speaking, and another saint said unto that certain *saint* which spake, How long *shall be* the vision *concerning* the daily *sacrifice*, and the transgression of desolation, to give both the sanctuary and the host to be trodden under foot? ¹⁴ And he said unto me, Unto two thousand and three hundred days; then shall the sanctuary be cleansed.

Daniel overhears the conversation between two angels to learn that the daily sacrifice being taken away and the desolation of the sanctuary will last for 2300 days. The prophetic year is 360 days. Seven prophetic years would by 2520 days. The difference is 220 days. This period of 220 days would probably be the time period between the start of the seventieth week and the restarting of the sacrificial system in the rebuilt temple. The temple would be rebuilt in this seven months and ten days period. The unbelievers of Israel will go back to these Mosaic sacrifices which no longer have value (Heb. 6:1-4). The believing remnant of Israel during the tribulation period will go to Christ "without the camp…" That is – they will go outside of the camp of Israel and the Old Covenant to put their trust in Christ as their real high priest who "…by his own blood he entered in once into the holy place, having obtained eternal redemption for us." (Heb 9:12). They will be going on to the New Covenant in the shed blood of their Messiah. The sanctuary will be profaned when the antichrist suspends the sacrifices in the middle of the week "…so that he as God sitteth in the temple of God showing himself that he is God…" (2Thess 2:4). This is the abomination of desolation spoken by our Lord in Matthew 24:15. The cleansing of the sanctuary happens when the Lord returns to destroy the antichrist and to enter the sanctuary Himself. Zechariah 14 describes that arrival of the Lord to save Israel. Israel's New Covenant shall then be instituted (Isa. 1:27; 45:25; Rom. 11:26-27; Jer. 31:31; Ezek. 36:24-27; etc.). Christ will then purify the sons of Levi that they might offer pure sacrifices during the Millennial reign. These pure sacrifices will be done as a memorial of the blood of Christ (Mal. 3:3 & 4)

Daniel 8:15-17

¹⁵ And it came to pass, when I, *even* I Daniel, had seen the vision, and sought for the meaning, then, behold, there stood before me as the appearance of a man. ¹⁶ And I heard a man's voice between *the banks of* Ulai, which called, and said, Gabriel, make this *man* to understand the vision. ¹⁷ So he came near where I stood: and when he came, I was afraid, and fell upon my face: but he said unto me, Understand, O son of man: for at the time of the end *shall be* the vision.

Daniel is informed that the vision is not for any near term event but is rather for a future end time event. The time defined in the Bible as "…the end…" is the end of the Gentile dominion of the world that began at Babel in Genesis Chapter 10 and the end of the "…times of the Gentiles" that began with the

Babylonian captivity of Israel. In Luke 21:24, the Lord tells us that Jerusalem shall be trodden down of the Gentiles until the times of the Gentiles be fulfilled. That fulfillment will be when Christ returns to set up His kingdom.

Daniel 8:18-19

[18] Now as he was speaking with me, I was in a deep sleep on my face toward the ground: but he touched me, and set me upright. [19] And he said, Behold, I will make thee know what shall be in the last end of the indignation: for at the time appointed the end *shall be.*

The expression "at the time appointed the end shall be." Takes us to Habakkuk 2:1-4 " I will stand upon my watch, and set me upon the tower, and will watch to see what he will say unto me, and what I shall answer when I am reproved. [2] And the LORD answered me, and said, Write the vision, and make *it* plain upon tables, that he may run that readeth it. [3] For the vision *is* yet for an appointed time, but at the end it shall speak, and not lie: though it tarry, wait for it; because it will surely come, it will not tarry. [4] Behold, his soul *which* is lifted up is not upright in him: but the just shall live by his faith." The key to understanding the expression is in the words "at the end it shall speak." The details will be apparent at the time that the prophecy will be fulfilled.

The Medo-Persian and Greek Empires

Daniel 8: 20-25

[20] The ram which thou sawest having *two* horns *are* the kings of Media and Persia. [21] And the rough goat *is* the king of Grecia: and the great horn that *is* between his eyes *is* the first king. [22] Now that being broken, whereas four stood up for it, four kingdoms shall stand up out of the nation, but not in his power. [23] And in the latter time of their kingdom, when the transgressors are come to the full, a king of fierce countenance, and understanding dark sentences, shall stand up. [24] And his power shall be mighty, but not by his own power: and he shall destroy wonderfully, and shall prosper, and practice, and shall destroy the mighty and the holy people. [25] And through his policy also he shall cause craft to prosper in his hand; and he shall magnify *himself* in his heart, and by peace shall destroy many: he shall also stand up against the Prince of princes; but he shall be broken without hand.

Verse 23 says that in the latter times of their kingdom (singular) a king of fierce countenance and understanding dark sentences shall stand up. This will be the antichrist. It will not happen until the transgressors are come to the full. This person will be the vile person of Daniel 11:21 who will have understanding of dark sentences. He will bring in great deception such that he comes "[10] …with all deceivableness of unrighteousness in them that perish; because they received not the love of the truth, that they might be saved." (2Thess. 2:10) Through his policy he shall cause craft to prosper in his hand – this will be witchcraft by which he displays "…all power and signs and lying wonders." By peace he shall destroy many. Daniel 11:21 says that "…he shall come in peaceably, and obtain the kingdom by flatteries." He shall be mighty but not by his own power – his power is given to him by none other that Satan. He will receive from Satan what Satan offered to the Lord but which the Lord would not take (Matt. 4:8 & 9). He magnifies himself in his heart (2Thess. 2:1-4) and stands up against the Prince of princes (Rev. 17:14; 19:16). However, he shall be broken without hand. It will not be a mortal human hand that breaks him but the Lord himself (Dan. 2:34, 35, 44, 45; 7:26; 11:45; Rev.19:19 & 20).

Daniel a closed book but the Revelation an Open Book

Daniel 8:26-27

[26] And the vision of the evening and the morning which was told *is* true: wherefore shut thou up the vision; for it *shall be* for many days. [27] And I Daniel fainted, and was sick *certain* days; afterward I rose up, and did the king's business; and I was astonished at the vision, but none understood *it*.

Daniel is told to shut up the vision. John was told not to shut up the vision (Rev. 22:10) that he received from the Lord. Daniel is a closed book because there will need to be more knowledge (more revelation) given before the book can be understood. With the Book of the Revelation, that additional knowledge is now available.

Daniel Chapter 8: Study Guide Questions

1. Where was Daniel when the events of Chapter 8 transpired?

2. What empire does the ram of Verses 1-4 represent? Who do the two horns represent?

3. Who does the higher horn represent?

4. Identify the He Goat of Verses 5-8.

5. From what direction does the He Goat come? Why does he not touch the ground?

6. What is the significance of the He Goat breaking the two horns of the Ram?

7. What does the breaking of the great horn of the He Goat symbolize? Why do four horns take its place? Who do the four horns represent?

8. Who is the Little Horn of verse 9? Have we met him before? What does it mean that he "Waxed great even to the host of heaven?" Who are the hosts of heaven? What does it mean that he cast down some of the host and the stars to the ground? Does Revelation 12:7-10 relate to this? What is the pleasant land of verse 9?

9. Who is the "prince of the host?" How did he magnify himself to the prince of the host?

10. What is the taking away of the daily sacrifice?

11. What is the transgression of Verse 13 talking bout?

12. What does it mean that the little horn practiced and prospered?

13. What is the significance of the 2300 days of Verse 14? Can we calculate from this how far into the seventieth week of Daniel Chapter 9 that the temple is rebuilt?

14. What is the transgression of desolation?

15. In Verse 12, Gabriel gives Daniel the time frame for this vision. What is that time frame?

16. Lay out the sequence of events summarized in Verses 20-26.

17. Who is the king of fierce continence in Verse 23? What does it mean that he understands dark sentences?

18. According to Verse 27, who will understand the vision?

Chapter 9
The Seventy Weeks to the Establishing of the Kingdom

The Book of the Revelation covers a period of time in the future that is often called the "Seventieth week of Daniel." It is so called because of an amazing passage in Daniel chapter 9. In Daniel 9:24 – 27 The angel Gabriel is sent by God to answer Daniel's question regarding what will happen when the seventy years of captivity is fulfilled. The seventy years of captivity is foretold in Jeremiah 25:11,

> "11 And this whole land shall be a desolation, *and* an astonishment; and these nations shall serve the king of Babylon seventy years." (Jeremiah 25:11)

Daniel had a copy of the Book of Jeremiah and had understanding of the seventy years of captivity from that book (Dan. 9:2). Daniel was praying to the Lord for information as to what will happen now that the seventy years were almost up. Daniel was wondering what will happen when the nation returned to the land. In Daniel Chapter 9, we find Daniel confessing his sins and the sins of the nation. This is exactly what the nation was to do to get out from under the judgment that came upon them because of their disobedience. In Leviticus 26:14 thru 39 we find five different and successive courses of judgment that would come upon Israel for her sin and rebellion. The first course is in Leviticus 26:14-17. The second is found in Verses 18 to 20. The third is in Verses 21 & 22 and the fourth is in Verses 23 to 26. The fifth course is in Verse 27 through 34 and covers the captivity of the nation. Then in Verses 40 on in Leviticus Chapter 26 we find the instructions that the Lord gives to Israel as to how to get out from under the judgment. Note:

Leviticus 26:40-45
> "40 If they shall confess their iniquity, and the iniquity of their fathers, with their trespass which they trespassed against me, and that also they have walked contrary unto me; 41 And *that* I also have walked contrary unto them, and have brought them into the land of their enemies; if then their uncircumcised hearts be humbled, and they then accept of the punishment of their iniquity: 42 Then will I remember my covenant with Jacob, and also my covenant with Isaac, and also my covenant with Abraham will I remember; and I will remember the land. 43 The land also shall be left of them, and shall enjoy her Sabbaths, while she lieth desolate without them: and they shall accept of the punishment of their iniquity: because, even because they despised my judgments, and because their soul abhorred my statutes. 44 And yet for all that, when they be in the land of their enemies, I will not cast them away, neither will I abhor them, to destroy them utterly, and to break my covenant with them: for I *am* the LORD their God. 45 But I will for their sakes remember the covenant of their ancestors, whom I brought forth out of the land of Egypt in the sight of the heathen, that I might be their God: I *am* the LORD."

(Leviticus 26:40-45)

Israel's captivity in these Gentile Kingdoms is the result of the fifth of the five successive courses of judgment that would come on the nation for her failure to keep the Law of Moses. The five courses are spelled out in Leviticus Chapter 26. See C. I. Schofield's notes on that chapter for a lay out of those judgments. Israel's History can be traced by following the successive courses of judgment. The courses are as follows:

- First course   The Period covered by Judges, Ruth, and 1Samual Chapters 1 to 16

Note: The Davidic Kingdom is a bright interlude between the first and the second

- Second   Elijah's ministry covers the second period (1Kings 12 thru 22)
- Third   Elisha's ministry covers the third (2Kings 1 thru 10:31)
- Fourth   War between Israel and Judah (2Kings 10:32 thru 16:20)
- Fifth   Israel captive of Assyria - Isaiah's ministry to Judah (2Kings 17:1 thru the end of the Bible). The ministries of the writing prophets to Judah and Israel.

The fifth course is divided into five parts.

1. The Assyrian captivity of Israel and Babylonian captivity of Judah.
2. The return of a remnant to Jerusalem under the Medes and Persians.
3. The silence of God from Malachi's ministry to John the Baptist's under the Greco-Roman Empire.
4. Under Roman rule during the Gospels and Acts.

Note: The Dispensation of Grace is an interruption in the fifth course between the fourth and the fifth parts.

5. The Tribulation Period under the reign of the antichrist. The books of Hebrews thru the Revelation instruct Israel on how to get through the Tribulation and into the Kingdom.

The fifth course finally ends with the return of Jesus Christ to Israel to reign as King of Kings and Lord of Lords.

In Leviticus Chapter 26:40-45 we find how the nation can get out from under the judgments. If Israel would confess her sins before the Lord, he would bring Israel back and would bless the nation. This confessing of his sins and those of his people is what Daniel is doing here in the first verses of in Chapter 9 of Daniel. One day in the future, this will be the heart attitude of all of Israel -- and so all Israel will be saved as we read of it in Romans 11:25-27. It is not that God will override stubborn unbelief on the part of individual Israelites but rather that only believing Israelites will go into the Kingdom. What will result in "…all Israel being saved…" is going to be the purging of the threshing floor that John the Baptist spoke of in Matthew 3:12.

Daniel 9:1-3 (KJV)

[1] In the first year of Darius the son of Ahasuerus, of the seed of the Medes, which was made king over the realm of the Chaldeans; [2] In the first year of his reign I Daniel understood by books the number of the years, whereof the word of the LORD came to Jeremiah the prophet, that he would accomplish seventy years in the desolations of Jerusalem. [3] And I set my face unto the Lord God, to seek by prayer and supplications, with fasting, and sackcloth, and ashes:

Jeremiah was a contemporary of Daniel. Daniel apparently had a copy of the Book of Jeremiah. Jeremiah 25:11 tells about the seventy years of captivity. The Book of 2Chronicles closes with the start of the captivity.

Daniel 9:4-14

[4] And I prayed unto the LORD my God, and made my confession, and said, O Lord, the great and dreadful God, keeping the covenant and mercy to them that love him, and to them that keep his commandments; [5] We have sinned, and have committed iniquity, and have done wickedly, and have rebelled, even by departing from thy precepts and from thy judgments: [6] Neither have we hearkened unto thy servants the prophets, which spake in thy name to our kings, our princes, and our fathers,

and to all the people of the land. ^{7}O Lord, righteousness *belongeth* unto thee, but unto us confusion of faces, as at this day; to the men of Judah, and to the inhabitants of Jerusalem, and unto all Israel, *that are* near, and *that are* far off, through all the countries whither thou hast driven them, because of their trespass that they have trespassed against thee. ^{8}O Lord, to us *belongeth* confusion of face, to our kings, to our princes, and to our fathers, because we have sinned against thee. ^{9}To the Lord our God *belong* mercies and forgivenesses, though we have rebelled against him; ^{10}Neither have we obeyed the voice of the LORD our God, to walk in his laws, which he set before us by his servants the prophets. ^{11}Yea, all Israel have transgressed thy law, even by departing, that they might not obey thy voice; therefore the curse is poured upon us, and the oath that *is* written in the law of Moses the servant of God, because we have sinned against him. ^{12}And he hath confirmed his words, which he spake against us, and against our judges that judged us, by bringing upon us a great evil: for under the whole heaven hath not been done as hath been done upon Jerusalem. ^{13}As *it is* written in the law of Moses, all this evil is come upon us: yet made we not our prayer before the LORD our God, that we might turn from our iniquities, and understand thy truth. ^{14}Therefore hath the LORD watched upon the evil, and brought it upon us: for the LORD our God *is* righteous in all his works which he doeth: for we obeyed not his voice.

Here Daniel is referring back to the Law of Moses in Leviticus 26, where the LORD lays out five successive courses of judgments that would come upon Israel if they did not live up to the standard of the Law. In Isaiah 49:24-25, Israel is referred to as the "lawful captive." Israel who was to rule the world under her Messiah was held captive by Satan who was using the Law to hold Israel captive. This is the result of Israel failing to live up to her legal covenant of the Law of Moses. Daniel understands that what happened with the captivity was God's work of fulfilling His word to Israel and that God had confirmed His Word (Verse 12) by the captivity.

The five courses of judgment that Daniel is looking back over from Leviticus 26 are:
The first: Leviticus 26:14-17
- Diseases
- Crops will be eaten by their enemies
- They will be slain before their enemies
- They that hate them will reign over them
- They will lose courage to stand against their enemies

The second: Leviticus 26:18-20
- The pride of their power will be broken
- The land will not yield her increase
- Their trees will not yield their fruit

The third: Leviticus 26:21&22 (1Kings covers this period)
- Wild beasts will rob them of their children
- They will loose population
- Their highways will be unsafe and desolate

The fourth: Leviticus 26: 23-26 (2Kings chapters 1 thru 11 covers this period)
- God will bring a sword against Israel
- Pestilence against the cities
- They will be delivered into the hands of their enemies

- There will be hunger in the land

The fifth: Leviticus 26:27 (2Kings 17 and forward covers this)

- They will eat the flesh of their sons and daughters.
- God will destroy their idolatry.
- Their carcasses will lie upon the carcasses of their idols.
- Their cities will be waste, their sanctuaries desolate
- God will not receive their prayers.
- Their land will be desolate with their enemies living in it.
- They will be scattered among the Gentiles.
- Military powers of the Gentiles will keep them out of the land
- The land will then enjoy her Sabbaths

Daniel 9:15-19

"¹⁵ And now, O Lord our God, that hast brought thy people forth out of the land of Egypt with a mighty hand, and hast gotten thee renown, as at this day; we have sinned, we have done wickedly. ¹⁶ O Lord, according to all thy righteousness, I beseech thee, let thine anger and thy fury be turned away from thy city Jerusalem, thy holy mountain: because for our sins, and for the iniquities of our fathers, Jerusalem and thy people *are become* a reproach to all *that are* about us. ¹⁷ Now therefore, O our God, hear the prayer of thy servant, and his supplications, and cause thy face to shine upon thy sanctuary that is desolate, for the Lord's sake. ¹⁸ O my God, incline thine ear, and hear; open thine eyes, and behold our desolations, and the city which is called by thy name: for we do not present our supplications before thee for our righteousnesses, but for thy great mercies. ¹⁹ O Lord, hear; O Lord, forgive; O Lord, hearken and do; defer not, for thine own sake, O my God: for thy city and thy people are called by thy name.

Note Daniel's appeal to the LORD. He does not appeal to anything he has done to merit any grace or mercy but to the name of the LORD. His appeal is "…for the Lord's sake…" (Vs. 17), "for the city that is called by thy name…" and "…for thy great mercies…" (vs. 18), "for thine own sake…" and because "thy city and thy people are called by thy name (Vs. 19).

Daniel 9:20-23

²⁰ And whiles I *was* speaking, and praying, and confessing my sin and the sin of my people Israel, and presenting my supplication before the LORD my God for the holy mountain of my God; ²¹ Yea, whiles I *was* speaking in prayer, even the man Gabriel, whom I had seen in the vision at the beginning, being caused to fly swiftly, touched me about the time of the evening oblation. ²² And he informed *me*, and talked with me, and said, O Daniel, I am now come forth to give thee skill and understanding. ²³ At the beginning of thy supplications the commandment came forth, and I am come to shew *thee*; for thou *art* greatly beloved: therefore understand the matter, and consider the vision.

The man Gabriel comes to Daniel being sent by God to give Daniel information in answer to his prayer and supplication. Gabriel is an arch (chief) angel along with Michael. They are apparently the only two of the arch angels that remained faithful to the Lord when the others defected to follow Lucifer in rebellion against God (Dan. 10:21).

The Prophecy of the Seventy Weeks

Daniel 9:24

> [24] Seventy weeks are determined upon thy people and upon thy holy city, to finish the transgression, and to make an end of sins, and to make reconciliation for iniquity, and to bring in everlasting righteousness, and to seal up the vision and prophecy, and to anoint the most Holy.

Daniel is told that though Israel was captive for seventy years, it will take seventy weeks or seven times seventy years to bring in the promised kingdom. A week in scripture can be any unit of seven. Genesis 29:18 and 27 illustrates how a week is used to represent seven years. The seventy weeks would be 490 years of 360 days (a prophetic year) each. He then lists what will be accomplished at the end of the seventy weeks:

- "To finish the transgression," (Matt. 1:21; 1Jonn 3:8). Israel's transgression of the Law will be over. This will be the result of the work of her Messiah who will "...save his people form their sins." (Matt. 1:21).

- "And to make an end of sins," (Lamentations 4:22; Col. 2:14; Heb. 9:26; 10:14). This will also be accomplished by Christ who suffered "...once in the end of the world... to put away sin by the sacrifice of himself." (Heb. 9:26). "For by one offering he hath perfected forever them that are sanctified." (Heb. 10:14). This will be accomplished through the New Covenant that God will make with Israel "And I will put my Spirit within you, and cause you to walk in my statutes, and ye shall keep my judgments, and do them." (Ezek. 36:27).

- "And to make reconciliation for iniquity," (Lev. 8:15; Isa 53:10; Rom 5:10; 2Cor 5:18-20; Col 1:20) God's justice must be satisfied. The penalty of sin must be paid. The blood of innocent animals covered sins and allowed God to remit the sins of those who brought the required sacrifice before the cross (Rom 3:25) but the sacrifice that cleared the account forever would be Christ's sacrifice of Himself (Rom.3:25; 2Cor. 5:18-21; Col. 1:20; Rom. 5:10).

- "And to bring in everlasting righteousness." (Isa. 51:6-8; 53:11; 56:1; Jer. 23:5,6; Rom. 3:21,23) "Behold a king shall reign in righteousness, and princes shall rule in judgment." Isa 32:1)

- "And to seal up the vision..." (Matt. 11:13; Luke. 24:25-27; 44, 45) The vision is in Chapter 8. "The vision is true: wherefore shut thou up the vision; for it shall be for many days." (Dan. 8:26).

- "And prophecy," (Acts 3:22) All prophecy must be fulfilled. "...All things must be fulfilled, which were written in the Law of Moses, and in the prophets, and in the Psalms, concerning me." (Luke 24:44)

- And to anoint the most Holy (Psalm 2:6; 45:7; Mark 1:24; Luke 1:35; Acts 3:14; Hebrews 7:26; Rev. 3:7) "The kingdoms of this world are become the kingdoms of our Lord and of his Christ; and he shall reign for ever and ever." (Rev. 11:15).

Daniel 9:25

[25] Know therefore and understand, *that* from the going forth of the commandment to restore and to build Jerusalem unto the Messiah the Prince *shall be* seven weeks, and threescore and two weeks: the street shall be built again, and the wall, even in troublous times.

The commandment to restore and to build Jerusalem is found in Nehemiah 2:1-8. For the student who would like to see the mathematics of this amazing prophecy, I would recommend the book "The Coming Prince" by Sir Robert Anderson published by Kregel Publishing. In that excellent study, Anderson does the math and shows conclusively that the 69th week ended on the very day that the Lord Jesus Christ rode into Jerusalem on a donkey. The first seven weeks are for the building of the walls in troublous times. At the end of the 69th week, Messiah arrives.

Daniel 9:26

> [26] And after threescore and two weeks shall Messiah be cut off, but not for himself: and the people of the prince that shall come shall destroy the city and the sanctuary; and the end thereof *shall be* with a flood, and unto the end of the war desolations are determined.

Messiah Arrives exactly on time at the end of the 69th week.

Note that it is <u>after</u> the three score and two weeks (for a total of 69 weeks) that Messiah is cut off – He is put to death (Psalm 22:15; Isa. 53:8; Luke 24:26). There is an undisclosed period of time between the end of the 69th week and the beginning of the seventieth. However, in Luke 13:8, our Lord defines that period of time as being one year in the parable of the fig tree. The fig tree in prophecy is a type of religion (as it was in Eden when Adam and Eve sewed fig leaves to cover their nakedness). As a side note: Remember that the Lord replaced that covering with coats of animal skins – a type of the blood of Christ as the real price of redemption. The three years in Luke 13:8 was the three years of the Lord's earthly ministry to Israel when the religion of Israel was not able to produce true repentance in the nation. Religious activity (represented by the fig tree) never could produce true repentance. It takes a heart conversion in faith to do that.

When our Lord ascended to heaven after His death burial, and resurrection, He was to sit until it was time for His Father to make His enemies His footstool (Psalm 110:1; Matt. 22:44; Heb. 1:13) One year after the end of the 69th week takes us to the stoning of Stephen. In Acts 7:56 Stephen sees Christ standing at the Father's right hand. That tells us that the year of Luke 13:8 was up and the Lord was going to bring the seventieth week of Daniel Chapter 9 upon the earth. The next thing according to the prophetic schedule was then to be the Tribulation (the seventieth week). The Lord did indeed return to earth on schedule. However, instead of bringing the seventieth week of Daniel 9 (the Tribulation Period), He instead came to save Saul of Tarsus – the man who was leading Israel's rejection of their Messiah. In doing so, the Lord interrupted the seventy weeks for a second time and put the entire prophetic program on hold so that He can introduce the mystery program into the earth. The mystery was kept a secret -- hid in God (1Cor. 2:7; Eph. 3:7; Rom. 16:25) and not revealed until the time was right. The time was right when Israel rejected the third offer (the third call to repentance) by rejecting the ministry of the Holy Spirit at Pentecost.

The mystery involves a new body of believers (a new elect agency) that is separate and distinct from Israel that has a destiny to live for the honor and glory of Christ in the heavens (2Cor. 5:1). The mystery program will run its course and end with the catching away (2Thess. 4:15) of the church, which is Christ's body to its destiny in heaven where it will reign and rule there (2Tim. 2:10-12) for the honor and glory of the Savior. With the rapture, the mystery program will be consummated and the prophetic program will be picked up again where God left off with it in Chapter 7 of Acts and the seventieth week of Daniel Chapter 9 will then start.

Israel's Covenant with Death

Daniel 9:27

> [27] And he shall confirm the covenant with many for one week: and in the midst of the week he shall cause the sacrifice and the oblation to cease, and for the overspreading of abominations he shall make *it* desolate, even until the consummation, and that determined shall be poured upon the desolate.

Comparing this with other Bible passages, we understand that the covenant in view here is the covenant with death that Israel will make with the antichrist (Isa. 28:15-18). The antichrist will make a covenant with the unbelieving nation of Israel which will enable Israel to rebuild her temple and reinstitute her temple service. In the midst of the week he will cause the sacrifice to cease. This will then be when he goes into the temple of God showing himself that he is God (2Thess. 2:4). This is what the Lord refers to in Matthew 24:15 as the abomination of desolation spoken by Daniel the prophet.

Daniel Chapter 9: Study Guide Questions

1. What passage in Jeremiah is Daniel studying as he prays here in Chapter 9 of Daniel?

2. What is Daniel praying for here?

3. Lay out the verses in Leviticus that talk about the five successive courses of judgments that will come upon Israel for their failure to keep the Law. What great event in prophecy does the fifth course cover?

4. Leviticus 26:40 tells Israel what they must do to get out from under the fifth course. What was it that would deliver them?

5. The Old Testament scriptures (the historical books) from first Samuel forward is laid out according to the five successive courses of judgment. List what portions of the historical books cover each along with the Major Prophets to each. Also list the five parts of the fifth course.

6. Why does: the passage, Isaiah 49:24 – 25, refer to Israel as the lawful captive?

7. In Verses 15 to 18, we see Daniel's appeal to the Lord for mercy and grace. Is this appeal based on any merit in Israel or is it is spite of any lack of merit?

8. Who according to verses 20 – 23 comes to give Daniel the information that he is looking for?

9. How many years are contained in the seventy weeks of verse 24? How do we know that?

10. List seven things that will be accomplished at the end of the seventy weeks. Have these things been accomplished yet? Why not?

11. According to verse 25, what event triggers the seventy weeks?

12. There are two breaks in the action in the seventy weeks. One after 7 weeks and the other after 69 weeks. What is significant about these two breaks?

13. What happens between the end of the 69th week and the beginning of the 70th week? Where would the Dispensation of grace fit into the action? Could anyone have known that before the revelation of the mystery was given to us through Paul?

14. Verse 27 talks about a covenant. What covenant is that?

Chapter 10
The Vision of the Glory of God

Daniel 10:1 (KJV)

[1] In the third year of Cyrus king of Persia a thing was revealed unto Daniel, whose name was called Belteshazzar; and the thing *was* true, but the time appointed *was* long: and he understood the thing, and had understanding of the vision.

Here in Chapters 10 thru 12 we have the last vision recorded in the Book of Daniel. Daniel had understanding of the vision and understood that the information conveyed by the vision is true. However, the time-frame as to when the events portrayed by the vision will be a long way off in the future from where he was at in history. Daniel is mourning but does not state the reason for his mourning. We can speculate as to the reason though. This is the third year of Cyrus' reign. It was in the first year of his reign that the command to restore Jerusalem was given (Ezra 1:1-4). Some had returned under Zerubbabal (Ezra 2:1-2). It would be some time yet before a group of Jews would return under Ezra and another group under Nehemiah (Nehemiah 2:1-10). Daniel likely was concerned that the Jews did not desire to return to the homeland, but became complacent in the land of their captivity.

Daniel 10:2-13

[2] In those days I Daniel was mourning three full weeks. [3] I ate no pleasant bread, neither came flesh nor wine in my mouth, neither did I anoint myself at all, till three whole weeks were fulfilled. [4] And in the four and twentieth day of the first month, as I was by the side of the great river, which *is* Hiddekel; [5] Then I lifted up mine eyes, and looked, and behold a certain man clothed in linen, whose loins *were* girded with fine gold of Uphaz: [6] His body also *was* like the beryl, and his face as the appearance of lightning, and his eyes as lamps of fire, and his arms and his feet like in colour to polished brass, and the voice of his words like the voice of a multitude. [7] And I Daniel alone saw the vision: for the men that were with me saw not the vision; but a great quaking fell upon them, so that they fled to hide themselves. [8] Therefore I was left alone, and saw this great vision, and there remained no strength in me: for my comeliness was turned in me into corruption, and I retained no strength. [9] Yet heard I the voice of his words: and when I heard the voice of his words, then was I in a deep sleep on my face, and my face toward the ground. [10] And, behold, an hand touched me, which set me upon my knees and *upon* the palms of my hands. [11] And he said unto me, O Daniel, a man greatly beloved, understand the words that I speak unto thee, and stand upright: for unto thee am I now sent. And when he had spoken this word unto me, I stood trembling. [12] Then said he unto me, Fear not, Daniel: for from the first day that thou didst set thine heart to understand, and to chasten thyself before thy God, thy words were heard, and I am come for thy words. [13] But the prince of the kingdom of Persia withstood me one and twenty days: but, lo, Michael, one of the chief princes, came to help me; and I remained there with the kings of Persia.

The river Hiddekel is the Tigris River. There are many questions that we must answer for ourselves in this passage of scripture. One would be: Is there one heavenly visitor or two? The second question is: Who is he? Each reader will have to come to his own conclusion on this, but I believe that there are two separate men in this vision. The first is Christ in His transfigured (Pre-incarnate) form much like how Peter, James and John saw Him in Matthew 17:1-4. The description that we have of him in Verses 5 & 6 is strikingly similar to that given in Revelation 1:12-16 when John saw him in glory. The effect of the experience of seeing this heavenly visitor on Daniel and those that were with him was essentially the same as it was on Paul and them that were with him on the road to Damascus in Acts Chapter 9. Daniel apparently lapses into an unconscious state face down on the ground. It is then that another heavenly visitor arrives to bring him to consciousness. This second visitor is likely the angel Gabriel who Daniel met earlier in chapter 8 verse 16 and again in Chapter 9, Verse 21.

Gabriel's Message

What Gabriel tells Daniel is very informative of what goes on behind the scenes of what we can see in this world of events in heaven that influence what happens here. Gabriel is sent to give Daniel information on the kingdom of Persia and the Greek empire that will supersede it. There is a conflict that was going on in the heavens that prevented Gabriel from getting through to deliver the message to Daniel. There were satanic hosts that did not want the message delivered. An angelic creature (known here as the prince of the kingdom of Persia) withstood him for 21 days. There was then a king of Persia who was then Cyrus reigning on the earth. However, there was an angelic creature that was behind the human king of Persia. We see a similar situation in Isaiah 14 where in verse 4 the king of Babylon is being addressed but then in verse 14 of that chapter the text switches to the spirit creature that was behind him. The "they" of Daniel 4:25 are likely these angelic creatures. The "watchers" of Daniel 4:17 are these angels who influence the affairs on earth. In this we see that there are apparently only two of the chief angels that stayed faithful to God – Michael (who is Israel's prince) and the one speaking (who we presume to be Gabriel). It is apparent that the angelic hosts are arrayed in rank and authority as are people on earth. We see this in passages like Colossians 1:16 and Ephesians 6:12 which speak of thrones, dominions, principalities and powers both in heaven and in earth.

Daniel 10:14-19

> [14] Now I am come to make thee understand what shall befall thy people in the latter days: for yet the vision *is* for *many* days. [15] And when he had spoken such words unto me, I set my face toward the ground, and I became dumb. [16] And, behold, *one* like the similitude of the sons of men touched my lips: then I opened my mouth, and spake, and said unto him that stood before me, O my lord, by the vision my sorrows are turned upon me, and I have retained no strength. [17] For how can the servant of this my lord talk with this my lord? For as for me, straightway there remained no strength in me, neither is there breath left in me. [18] Then there came again and touched me *one* like the appearance of a man, and he strengthened me, [19] And said, O man greatly beloved, fear not: peace *be* unto thee, be strong, yea, be strong. And when he had spoken unto me, I was strengthened, and said, Let my lord speak; for thou hast strengthened me.

Before going into the content of the message, some observations are in order here. In verses 16 and 17 we see that the experience of the encounter with the angel left him without strength, it left him speechless, and it took his breath away. As we consider what Paul tells us members of the Body of Christ, we understand that there will have to be a very significant change in our nature at the rapture because we find that we shall actually judge angels (1Cor. 6:3).

Gabriel is telling Daniel what will befall his people in the latter days. This is information on the fate of Israel in the end times. Daniel is told that it is going to be many days (a long time into the future) before the details are realized.

Daniel 10:20-21

²⁰ Then said he, Knowest thou wherefore I come unto thee? and now will I return to fight with the prince of Persia: and when I am gone forth, lo, the prince of Grecia shall come. ²¹ But I will shew thee that which is noted in the scripture of truth: and *there is* none that holdeth with me in these things, but Michael your prince.

After Gabriel tells Daniel what will happen to Israel in the latter days, he will go and contend with the prince of Persia and after that, the prince of Grecia (Greece) will come. Michael is apparently the commander in chief of the armies of heaven. We see him in Revelation 12:7 involved in purging heaven of Satan and his angels. As we go to the Pauline Epistles on the subject of angelic intervention in the affairs of men, we essentially find none. Rather, what we find is that angels are learning about the wisdom of God as they observe the life changing effect of the gospel of grace on our lives today as believers are saved by grace through faith apart from works.

Daniel Chapter 10: Study Guide Questions

1. What is the common theme running through all of the last three chapters (Chapters 10 – 12) of Daniel? In what year of Cyrus' reign did the commandment to restore Jerusalem go forth? What was the time frame in Cyrus' reign in which this last of Daniel's visions is set?

2. Was this vision about a near term event or was the fulfillment in the distant future?

3. How many men appeared to Daniel in this event? Who was the first? Who was the second?

4. According to Verse 2, how many weeks was Daniel in mourning? What was he mourning? Who withstood Gabriel that he couldn't get through with the message for three weeks? Who came to help Gabriel so that he could get the message through to Daniel?

5. Who was the prince of Persia in the encounter in the angelic world? Who is the king of Persia in this narrative?

6. According to Verse 14, what people is this message all about?

7. Who is the prince of Persia in Verse 20? Who is the prince of Grecia? Who is Israel's prince? Are these princes human or angelic?

Chapter 11
From Darius to the Man of Sin

Daniel 11:1 (KJV)

¹ Also I in the first year of Darius the Mede, *even* I, stood to confirm and to strengthen him.

The speaker here is the angel (who I believe is Gabriel). Darius was reigning when Daniel was thrown into the lion's den in Chapter 6. Darius had spent the night in anxiety after having tried unsuccessfully to deliver Daniel from the lions den. It is interesting to note Darius' words "Thy God whom thou servest continually, he will deliver thee." (Dan. 6:16). Darius apparently was converted to faith in the true God through Daniel's testimony. Daniel told him in the morning "My God hath sent his angel and hath shut the lions' mouths that they have not hurt me: forasmuch as before him innocency was found in me; and also before thee, O king, have I done no hurt" (Dan 6:22).

Daniel 11:2-4

² And now will I shew thee the truth. Behold, there shall stand up yet three kings in Persia; and the fourth shall be far richer than *they* all: and by his strength through his riches he shall stir up all against the realm of Grecia. ³ And a mighty king shall stand up, that shall rule with great dominion, and do according to his will. ⁴ And when he shall stand up, his kingdom shall be broken, and shall be divided toward the four winds of heaven; and not to his posterity, nor according to his dominion which he ruled: for his kingdom shall be plucked up, even for others beside those.

This chapter of Daniel is history that is prewritten by the one that knows the future. Verse 2 says that there will be yet three kings in Persia but then there is a fourth who will be wealthier than the others. There will be four kings in all. The fourth is Xerxes who is the Ahaesuerus of the Book of Esther. The four kings that the angel refers to are:

Cambyses	529 BC
Pseudo-Smerdis	522 BC
Darius Hystaspis	521 BC
Xerxes	480 BC

The mighty king of verse 3 is Alexander the Great of Greece. He came to power in about 335 BC and died in 323 BC. After his death the kingdom was divided between his four generals. The four divisions were:

Cassander took Macedonia

Lysimachus took Asia Minor (Modern day Turkey)

Seleucus Nicator took Syria (Collectively known as the king of the north)

Ptolemy took Egypt (Collectively known as the king of the south)

These families warred against each other over the next several centuries. The Seleucid family of Syria and the Ptolemy family in Egypt were particularly known for being at war with each other. From Verse 5 thru Verse 20, the narrative is about the warfare and interaction between the two, with the King of Egypt being the king of the south and the Syrian king being the king of the north. The prophecy of this interaction is very detailed and was fulfilled exactly as prophesied. For those interested in following the fulfillment of this prophecy, the reader should consult the book "The Prophet Daniel" by Arno Gabelein, the Book "The

<u>Coming Prince</u>" by Sir Robert Anderson or the material by Dwight Pentecost. The material "<u>Through the Bible</u>" by J. Vernon McGee also gives an excellent treatment of the information in these verses.

Ongoing Warfare between Syria and Egypt in the Inter-testament Period

Daniel 11:5-20

[5] And the king of the south shall be strong, and *one* of his princes; and he shall be strong above him, and have dominion; his dominion *shall be* a great dominion. [6] And in the end of years they shall join themselves together; for the king's daughter of the south shall come to the king of the north to make an agreement: but she shall not retain the power of the arm; neither shall he stand, nor his arm: but she shall be given up, and they that brought her, and he that begat her, and he that strengthened her in *these* times. [7] But out of a branch of her roots shall *one* stand up in his estate, which shall come with an army, and shall enter into the fortress of the king of the north, and shall deal against them, and shall prevail: [8] And shall also carry captives into Egypt their gods, with their princes, *and* with their precious vessels of silver and of gold; and he shall continue *more* years than the king of the north. [9] So the king of the south shall come into *his* kingdom, and shall return into his own land. [10] But his sons shall be stirred up, and shall assemble a multitude of great forces: and *one* shall certainly come, and overflow, and pass through: then shall he return, and be stirred up, *even* to his fortress. [11] And the king of the south shall be moved with choler, and shall come forth and fight with him, *even* with the king of the north: and he shall set forth a great multitude; but the multitude shall be given into his hand.

[12] *And* when he hath taken away the multitude, his heart shall be lifted up; and he shall cast down *many* ten thousands: but he shall not be strengthened *by it*. [13] For the king of the north shall return, and shall set forth a multitude greater than the former, and shall certainly come after certain years with a great army and with much riches. [14] And in those times there shall many stand up against the king of the south: also the robbers of thy people shall exalt themselves to establish the vision; but they shall fall. [15] So the king of the north shall come, and cast up a mount, and take the most fenced cities: and the arms of the south shall not withstand, neither his chosen people, neither *shall there be any* strength to withstand. [16] But he that cometh against him shall do according to his own will, and none shall stand before him: and he shall stand in the glorious land, which by his hand shall be consumed. [17] He shall also set his face to enter with the strength of his whole kingdom, and upright ones with him; thus shall he do: and he shall give him the daughter of women, corrupting her: but she shall not stand *on his side*, neither be for him. [18] After this shall he turn his face unto the isles, and shall take many: but a prince for his own behalf shall cause the reproach offered by him to cease; without his own reproach he shall cause *it* to turn upon him. [19] Then he shall turn his face toward the fort of his own land: but he shall stumble and fall, and not be found. [20] Then shall stand up in his estate a raiser of taxes *in* the glory of the kingdom: but within few days he shall be destroyed, neither in anger, nor in battle.

The information given in Verses 3 through 20 was prophetic when it was given to Daniel. However, it is now history that has been fulfilled as stated. The information presented in Verses 20 through the end of the chapter is often presented as referring to Anticus Epiphanes. It may be that the career of Anticus is also in view as a near term fulfillment because it does fit his career and exploits well. However, the ultimate fulfillment of this prophecy is in the career of the antichrist. Clearly, the vile person in Verse 20 and on is the antichrist, not Anticus Epiphanes. Comparing scripture with scripture it becomes clear that he (the antichrist is the one ultimately in view in this prophecy.

The Vile Person of the End Times

Daniel 11:21-22

21 And in his estate shall stand up a vile person, to whom they shall not give the honour of the kingdom: but he shall come in peaceably, and obtain the kingdom by flatteries. 22 And with the arms of a flood shall they be overflown from before him, and shall be broken; yea, also the prince of the covenant.

Verse 21 takes us through to the end times. In Daniel 8:25 the king of fierce countenance who comes out of the Greek (actually the Greco-Roman empire) empire in the last days will "…by peace…destroy many." In Revelation 6:2 the rider of the white horse (the antichrist) has a bow but no arrows. He goes forth "conquering, and to conquer." This is symbolic of the tactic of using peace to destroy nations.

He shall come in peaceably "The words of his mouth were smoother than butter, but war was in his heart; his words were softer than oil, yet were they drawn swords." (Psalm 55:21) In 2Samuel 15:2-6 Absalom used the tactic of deceit to steal the hearts of the people of Israel and use peace to attempt to overthrow his father David.

Daniel 11:23-26

23 And after the league made with him he shall work deceitfully: for he shall come up, and shall become strong with a small people. 24 He shall enter peaceably even upon the fattest places of the province; and he shall do that which his fathers have not done, nor his fathers' fathers; he shall scatter among them the prey, and spoil, and riches: yea, and he shall forecast his devices against the strong holds, even for a time. 25 And he shall stir up his power and his courage against the king of the south with a great army; and the king of the south shall be stirred up to battle with a very great and mighty army; but he shall not stand: for they shall forecast devices against him. 26 Yea, they that feed of the portion of his meat shall destroy him, and his army shall overflow: and many shall fall down slain.

The league of Verse 23 would be the ten nation confederacy of Psalm 83. "For they have consulted together with one consent: they are confederate against thee." (Psalm 83:5) Much of Bible prophecy has both a near and ultimate fulfillment. Isaiah's words in Isaiah 8:5-14 is a case in point. In the end times, just as in Isaiah's day, Israel (the unbelieving nation) will join in a covenant with the antichrist (the man called "the Assyrian") for seven years, but he will work deceitfully. "…he shall scatter among them the prey, and spoil, and riches: yea, and he shall forecast his devices against the strong holds, even for a time." (Dan. 11:24) The antichrist makes a covenant with Israel in Daniel 9:27, but breaks the covenant in the middle of the week (the seven year period). The Lord refers to that covenant saying regarding Israel, "We have made a covenant with death, and with hell are we at agreement." (Isa. 28:15)

Daniel 11:27-30

[27] And both these kings' hearts *shall be* to do mischief, and they shall speak lies at one table; but it shall not prosper: for yet the end *shall be* at the time appointed. [28] Then shall he return into his land with great riches; and his heart *shall be* against the holy covenant; and he shall do *exploits*, and return to his own land. [29] At the time appointed he shall return, and come toward the south; but it shall not be as the former, or as the latter. [30] For the ships of Chittim shall come against him: therefore he shall be grieved, and return, and have indignation against the holy covenant: so shall he do; he shall even return, and have intelligence with them that forsake the holy covenant.

The antichrist's "heart shall be against the holy covenant..." (Verse 28) The holy covenant is the New Covenant the Lord makes with Israel as the blood of the New Covenant that purchases Israel's redemption. He will have intelligence with them that forsake the holy covenant (Verse. 30). These are Jews who do not put their trust in the blood of Christ. The writer of Hebrews speaks of them in Hebrews 2:3: "How shall we escape if we neglect so great salvation; which at the first began to be spoken by the Lord, and was confirmed unto us by them that heard him;"

Daniel 11:31-32

[31] And arms shall stand on his part, and they shall pollute the sanctuary of strength, and shall take away the daily *sacrifice*, and they shall place the abomination that maketh desolate. [32] And such as do wickedly against the covenant shall he corrupt by flatteries: but the people that do know their God shall be strong, and do *exploits*.

The antichrist will pollute the sanctuary of strength when he takes away the daily sacrifice and sets himself up as God sitting in the temple of God. (2Thess. 2:3-4) The unbelievers of Israel will be taken in by the deception (2Thess. 2:10). At that time ". . . there shall arise false Christs, and false prophets, and shall shew great signs and wonders; insomuch that, if it were possible, they shall deceive the very elect." (Matt. 24:24)

Daniel 11:33-35

[33] And they that understand among the people shall instruct many: yet they shall fall by the sword, and by flame, by captivity, and by spoil, *many* days. [34] Now when they shall fall, they shall be holpen with a little help: but many shall cleave to them with flatteries. [35] And *some* of them of understanding shall fall, to try them, and to purge, and to make *them* white, *even* to the time of the end: because *it is* yet for a time appointed.

"They that understand..." in verse 33 are the believers who will instruct many. During the tribulation period, "the brother shall deliver up the brother to death, and the father the child: and the children shall rise up against their parents, and cause them to be put to death." (Matt.10:21) What a horrible time of deceit and deception that will be. The Lord tells his disciples that in that time ". . . whosoever killeth you will think that he doeth God service." (John 16:2) Isaiah 32:1-8 speaks of believers in that day. Thet will have understanding of what is really happening

"And the eyes of them that see shall not be dim, and the ears of them that hear shall hearken. The heart also of the rash shall understand knowledge, and the tongue of the stammering shall be ready to speak plainly." This is a quote from Isaiah 32:3-4. The next verses that follow are a reference to "the vile person" who is the antichrist. The often repeated warning in the Revelation regarding those times is: "…him that hath an ear to hear let him hear…" They that understand among the people [of Israel] shall instruct many. This is the commission that God gives to the twelve in Matthew 28:20. It will be carried out in the tribulation period by the 144,000 of Revelation 7:4; 14:1; etc.

"…Many shall cleave to them with flatteries." These will be the false prophets that the Lord warns about in Matthew 7:15. Peter warns of them also in 2Peter 2:1-3. There will be a woman in the tribulation period called Jezebel who will call herself a prophetess but who teaches idolatrous doctrine (Rev. 2:20) Paul speaks of such teachers that join themselves to believers by using "good words and fair speeches deceive the hearts of the simple" (Rom. 16:18).

Daniel 11:36-39

36 And the king shall do according to his will; and he shall exalt himself, and magnify himself above every god, and shall speak marvellous things against the God of gods, and shall prosper till the indignation be accomplished: for that that is determined shall be done. 37 Neither shall he regard the God of his fathers, nor the desire of women, nor regard any god: for he shall magnify himself above all. 38 But in his estate shall he honour the God of forces: and a god whom his fathers knew not shall he honour with gold, and silver, and with precious stones, and pleasant things. 39 Thus shall he do in the most strong holds with a strange god, whom he shall acknowledge *and* increase with glory: and he shall cause them to rule over many, and shall divide the land for gain.

The king (the antichrist) will be a self-willed king ("he shall do according to his will" – verse 36). The Lord Jesus Christ came to do His Father's will (John 5:30). The antichrist "…shall exalt himself." The Lord Jesus Christ humbled himself to exalt the Father (Phil. 2:5-8). The Holy Ghost came to exalt the Son (John 15:26). Each of the members of the Trinity exalts the other two. However the antichrist will "…magnify himself above every god and shall speak marvelous things against the God of gods." The arrogance of this man will be astonishing. He will "oppose and exalt himself above all that is called God, or that is worshipped; so that he as God sitteth in the temple of God, shewing himself that he is God." (2Thess. 2:4). His deceptive speech and his exploits will be convincing because "…all that dwell upon the earth shall worship him, whose names are not written in the book of life of the Lamb slain from the foundation of the world." (Rev. 13:8)

He will not regard the God of his fathers (Verse 37). This tells us that he will probably be of Jewish ancestry. He will not regard the desire of women – every Jewish woman considers the possibility that she would be the mother of the Messiah as the Scripture spoke regarding "the seed of the woman" crushing Satan's head. The words "But in his estate…" in Verse 38 is a reference to "…the God of his fathers" in verse 37. Instead of the God of his fathers he will honor the "God of forces: and a god whom his fathers knew not…" The "them" who rule in Verse 39 which he causes to rule are apparently the ten kings represented by the ten toes of Daniel 2:42 and the ten horns of Daniel 7:7, 20, 24, and Revelation 12:3. Isaiah 10: 5 addresses the antichrist calling him "O Assyrian, the rod of mine anger, and the staff in their hand is mine indignation. I will send him against an hypocritical nation… Are not my princes [the ten kings of Psalm 83] altogether kings?" It is apparent from Daniel 2:43 that these ten are demonic "…they shall mingle themselves with the seed of men; but they shall not cleave one to another, even as iron is not mixed with clay." We find iron in Scripture often associated with demonic activity influencing humanity.

Daniel 11:40-41

> [40] And at the time of the end shall the king of the south push at him: and the king of the north shall come against him like a whirlwind, with chariots, and with horsemen, and with many ships; and he shall enter into the countries, and shall overflow and pass over. [41] He shall enter also into the glorious land, and many *countries* shall be overthrown: but these shall escape out of his hand, *even* Edom, and Moab, and the chief of the children of Ammon.

In Verse 41, he shall enter into the glorious land -- the land of Israel. In this campaign, many countries in the Middle East are conquered, but Edom, Moab and sons of Ammon escape being under his control. These will likely be the hidden place where the woman in Revelation 12:6 (who represents the nation of Israel) flees to escape the wrath of the great red dragon of Revelation 12:3. The woman (Israel) is hidden for 1260 days (Rev. 12:6) or 3.5 prophetic years of 360 days each. The woman (Israel) comprises the "hidden ones" of Psalm 83:3. Ezekiel 38:8-13 describes this invasion of the land of Israel.

Daniel 11:42-43

> [42] He shall stretch forth his hand also upon the countries: and the land of Egypt shall not escape. [43] But he shall have power over the treasures of gold and of silver, and over all the precious things of Egypt: and the Libyans and the Ethiopians *shall be* at his steps.

In Verses 40 through 45 we see the antichrist gaining many victories but the victories are only temporary. In Verse 45, we see him placing his palace in the glorious holy mountain. That would be Mount Zion. However, he will ultimately come to an end. He will be destroyed by the Lord Jesus Christ "…with the brightness of his coming." (2Thess. 2:8) Revelation 20:1-10 describes the ultimate destruction of the unholy trinity (the devil, the antichrist, and his prophet). Ezekiel 38:22-23 also describes the ultimate destruction of the devil and his work in the world.

Daniel 11:44-45

> [44] But tidings out of the east and out of the north shall trouble him: therefore he shall go forth with great fury to destroy, and utterly to make away many. [45] And he shall plant the tabernacles of his palace between the seas in the glorious holy mountain; yet he shall come to his end, and none shall help him.

The antichrist will be an irresistible conqueror as long as his career lasts. Here we see him establish his palace in Jerusalem. It is probable that at this time his blasphemous act of Daniel 9:27; 12:11; Matthew 24:15; and 2Thessalonians 2:4 happens. This marks the beginning of the second half of the week (the three and a half years of Daniel 7:25; 12:7, 11; and Revelation 13:5).

Daniel Chapter 11: Study Guide Questions

1. Who, according to Verse 1, strengthened Darius the Mede?

2. According to Verse 2, how many kings would follow Cyrus on the throne of Persia? List the four kings of Persia and the date of their ascension.

3. Who is the mighty king of Verse 3?

4. List the fourfold division of Alexander's kingdom.

5. Who is the "vile person" of Verse 21? Is Verse 21 history or prophecy? What does it mean "…He shall come in peaceably?"

6. What is the league that Verse 23 talks about?

7. What is "…the holy covenant" to which Verse 30 refers? Who are "…they that forsake the holy covenant?" How does this relate to the passage in Hebrews 2:3?

8. What does Verse 31 foresee with the words "…they shall pollute the sanctuary of strength?" Is there a Pauline passage that also addresses this?

9. Who are "…they that understand" in Verse 33?

10. In Verse 34 we read "many shall cleave to them with flatteries…"? Who are these people that cleave to Israel with flatteries?

11. In Verse 39 we see that the antichrist causes people referred to as "them" to rule over many. Who are the "them"?

12. According to Verse 41, there are three middle-eastern countries that escape being taken over by the antichrist. Which countries are they?

Daniel Chapter 12
Two Resurrections of Prophecy and the Last Message to Daniel

Daniel 12:1 (KJV)

[1] And at that time shall Michael stand up, the great prince which standeth for the children of thy people: and there shall be a time of trouble, such as never was since there was a nation *even* to that same time: and at that time thy people shall be delivered, every one that shall be found written in the book.

The book referred to here in Verse 1 is the Book of Life. The Book of Life is a list of the names of the elect whether it be the elect of the age of the Patriarchs, the elect of Israel, or the elect of the church, the body of Christ. Your name (as a member of the Body of Christ) will not be taken out of the Book of Life. Passages that talk about removing names are talking about another book – the Book of Israel's national blessings under their covenants. The following are some of the passages that address these blessings. Israel will have to endure to the end of the tribulation period (Matt. 10:22) to enter these blessings.

Ezekiel 13:8 & 9 "[8]Therefore thus saith the Lord GOD; Because ye have spoken vanity, and seen lies, therefore, behold, I *am* against you, saith the Lord GOD. [9] And mine hand shall be upon the prophets that see vanity, and that divine lies: they shall not be in the assembly of my people, neither shall they be written in the writing of the house of Israel, neither shall they enter into the land of Israel; and ye shall know that I *am* the Lord GOD."

Psalm 69:28 "[28] Let them be blotted out of the book of the living, and not be written with the righteous."

Isaiah 4:3 "[3] And it shall come to pass, *that he that is* left in Zion, and *he that* remaineth in Jerusalem, shall be called holy, *even* every one that is written among the living in Jerusalem:"

The reference to Michael is the arch angel Michael. The time frame in view here is the time of the end when the war in heaven of Revelation 12:7 breaks out. When God starts to put down all rebellion, He starts in the heavens. "[7] And there was war in heaven: Michael and his angels fought against the dragon; and the dragon fought and his angels, [8] And prevailed not; neither was their place found any more in heaven. [9] And the great dragon was cast out, that old serpent, called the Devil, and Satan, which deceiveth the whole world: he was cast out into the earth, and his angels were cast out with him. [10] And I heard a loud voice saying in heaven, Now is come salvation, and strength, and the kingdom of our God, and the power of his Christ: for the accuser of our brethren is cast down, which accused them before our God day and night. [11] And they overcame him by the blood of the Lamb, and by the word of their testimony; and they loved not their lives unto the death." (Revelation 12:6-11).

In Isaiah 34:5 we see another prophecy of this event in heaven: "[4] And all the host of heaven shall be dissolved, and the heavens shall be rolled together as a scroll: and all their host shall fall down, as the leaf falleth off from the vine, and as a falling *fig* from the fig tree. [5] For my sword shall be bathed in heaven: behold, it shall come down upon Idumea, and upon the people of my curse, to judgment. [6] The sword of the LORD is filled with blood, it is made fat with fatness, *and* with the blood of lambs and goats, with the fat of the kidneys of rams: for the LORD hath a sacrifice in Bozrah, and a great slaughter in the land of Idumea. [7] And the unicorns shall come down with them, and the bullocks with the bulls; and their land shall be soaked with blood, and their dust made fat with fatness. [8] For *it is* the day of the LORD'S vengence, *and* the year of recompences for the controversy of Zion." (Isa. 334:4-8)

From Daniel 11:21 on to the end of the book, everything deals with the time of the end when Israel will be delivered from her enemies.

Daniel 12:2

[2] And many of them that sleep in the dust of the earth shall awake, some to everlasting life, and some to shame *and* everlasting contempt.

There are two resurrections in view in prophecy. There is the resurrection of the just and another of the unjust (Acts 24:15). In the Old Testament, people were regarded as just or unjust depending upon whether they walked according to the Law of Moses or not. In the case of those who lived before the Law they were just or unjust depending on whether they walked according to what God had revealed to them at that time. In the Book of the Revelation, we see these two resurrections separated by 1000 years (Rev. 20:5-6). The Old Testament saints (believers before the saving of Saul of Tarsus) will be raised in the first resurrection of Revelation 20. The resurrection of the lost of the ages is described in Revelation 20:12-15 where "The dead stand before God…" Note that they are raised bodily from the dead but they are still regarded as "dead". The resurrection of members of the church, the body of Christ, is not in view in any of the passages that deal with Israel (as this passage in Daniel does). That (the resurrection of members of the Body of Christ) is the subject of the mystery that was hid in God until it was revealed by Jesus Christ through the apostle Paul. The resurrection of the Body of Christ takes place at the catching away of the church (1Cor. 15:51; 1Thess. 4:15) at least seven years before the resurrection of the just of prophecy.

Daniel 12:3-4

[3] And they that be wise shall shine as the brightness of the firmament; and they that turn many to righteousness as the stars for ever and ever. [4] But thou, O Daniel, shut up the words, and seal the book, *even* to the time of the end: many shall run to and fro, and knowledge shall be increased.

Daniel is told here to seal the book. The Book of Daniel is a sealed book because there is more information that is needed to enable people to understand the book. John is told in the Revelation to "Seal not the sayings of the prophecy of this book for the time is at hand." (Rev. 22:10). Daniel is told that men shall run to and from looking for light and revelation. The knowledge that will increase after the closing of the Book of Daniel is knowledge of the prophetic program with Israel. This added knowledge is given in the four gospels and the Books of Hebrews thru the Book of the Revelation.

Daniel 12: 5-7

[5] Then I Daniel looked, and, behold, there stood other two, the one on this side of the bank of the river, and the other on that side of the bank of the river. [6] And *one* said to the man clothed in linen, which *was* upon the waters of the river, How long *shall it be to* the end of these wonders? [7] And I heard the man clothed in linen, which *was* upon the waters of the river, when he held up his right

hand and his left hand unto heaven, and sware by him that liveth for ever that *it shall be* for a time, times, and an half; and when he shall have accomplished to scatter the power of the holy people, all these *things* shall be finished.

The man clothed with linen reminds us of the mighty angel in Revelation 10:1-2 who was clothed with a cloud and had a rainbow around his head and his face as the sun and his feet as pillars of fire. That angel lifted up his hand to heaven also. That angel in Revelation 10, if he is not Christ personally, he certainly represents Christ. The message of the angel in Revelation 10 is "…that there should be time no longer…" That is to say, the time of the Gentile dominion of the earth is up and Christ is coming to take possession of the planet earth.

The time period described as "… a time, times, and half…" is the three and one half years of the second half of the seventieth week of Daniel Chapter 9. This is identical to the term "…a time and times, and the dividing of times…" in Daniel 7:25.

Daniel 12:8-11

[8] And I heard, but I understood not: then said I, O my Lord, what *shall be* the end of these *things?* [9] And he said, Go thy way, Daniel: for the words *are* closed up and sealed till the time of the end. [10] Many shall be purified, and made white, and tried; but the wicked shall do wickedly: and none of the wicked shall understand; but the wise shall understand. [11] And from the time *that* the daily *sacrifice* shall be taken away, and the abomination that maketh desolate set up, *there shall be* a thousand two hundred and ninety days.

If the abomination that Lord refers to in Matthew 24:15 and that the angel refers to in Daniel 9:23 & 27 happens in the middle of the week and there is 360 days/yr. x 3.5 years = 1260 days in the second half of the week, then the 1290 days ends 30 days after the close of the week.

Daniel 12:12-13

[12] Blessed *is* he that waiteth, and cometh to the thousand three hundred and five and thirty days. [13] But go thou thy way till the end *be*: for thou shalt rest, and stand in thy lot at the end of the days.

Daniel will stand in his lot (i.e. He will be raised from the dead) at the end of 1335 days. This would be 1335 days – 1260 days = 75 days after the close of the Tribulation period (the seventieth week). We would understand from this that the resurrection of the Old Testament saints will be at that time. The time frame for the resurrection of the church, the body of Christ, is not in view in the prophetic books such as the Book of Daniel, because our resurrection as members of the body of Christ is the subject of the mystery that was hid in God until it was revealed by the Lord Jesus Christ through Paul (1Cor. 2:7; 15:51; 1Thess. 4:16). Our resurrection happens when the church which is Christ's body is caught up to meet the Lord in the air (i.e. the unseen realm of heaven) before the seventieth week starts. The eternal destiny of the church the body of Christ is in the heavens (2Cor. 5:1). While the first half of the tribulation period unfolds on the earth, the judgment seat of Christ, in which the members of the Body of Christ are judged so that they can assume positions of responsibility there once Satan is expelled from heaven (Rev. 12:6) in the middle of the tribulation period. In the end, God will "reconcile all things unto Himself whether they be things in earth or things in heaven" (Col. 1:20). The nation of Israel is the elect agency by which He reconciles the things in earth to Himself. The church, which is Christ's body, is the elect agency by which he reconciles the things in heaven to Himself. In both cases, it is only through the blood of His cross that Christ is able to do that.

Daniel Chapter 12: Study Guide Questions

1. What is the book referred to in Verse 1?

2. What is the time frame of Verse 1 by the words "at that time…"? Who is Michael?

3. What two resurrections are in view in Verse 2? How many years transpire between them? Does either of these two resurrections include you? Where will you be while this drama goes on in the earth?

4. Why is it that Daniel is told to shut up the words of the book in Verse 3?

5. How much time is "time, and times, and half a time…" in Verse 7? We saw this terminology before in Daniel 7:25.

6. Verse 11 gives a benchmark of time – an event that triggers a time period. What is the trigger point?

7. There are three different time periods in Verses 11-13. They are 1260 days in length, 1290 days, and 1335 days. It appears that the setting up of the abomination of desolation is the trigger point for all three. What is that abomination of desolation? What happens at the end of each of these three time periods?

Appendix 1

For by him were all things created (Col. 1:16) He is before all things, and by Him all things consist	All things subdued unto Him (I Cor. 15:27) All things gathered together in Christ (Eph. 1:10)

History – God's record of the past		Declaring the end from ancient times (Isaiah 46:20) I have declared the former things from the beginning (Isaiah 48:3) In the latter days ye shall consider it perfectly (Jer. 23:20)		Prophecy – God's story of the future
	rst rebellion – Satan and angels ; Ezek. 28:140 rst judgment – chaos (Gen 1:2)		The final rebellion – Satan and men The final judgment – fire (Rev 21:8)	
	arth made ready for man 1:3-31)		The Earth a perfect habitat for man (Rev 22:1-7)	
	ubjection to Satan 3:1-19)		The subjecting of Satan (Rev 20:10)	
	arliest Gospel (Gen 3:15) rsal rebellion (Gen 6:1-7) nent by water (Noah –Gen 6:8-2: arth purged by water (Gen 7:17-: nments setup (Gen 9:5-7)		The Everlasting Gospel (Rev 14:6) Universal rebellion (Rev 20:8) Judgment by fire (2Pet 3:7) The floor purged (Mat 3:12) Kingdom setup Perfect Government	
	tion of Babylon ry invented (Gen 11:1-4) ns scattered (Gen 11:5-9)		Destruction of Babylon (Rev. 18:2) Idolatry ended Rev 9:20; 21:8) Nations gathered (Rev 16:4; 20:8)	
	mes of the Gentiles begins Ezra, Neh.)		The times of the Gentiles ends (Lk 21:24; Rev. 11:5)	
	rst advent of Christ to the mange		The second advent of Christ to the throne	
	pirit poured out 2:17) nd coming in view all of Israel		The Spirit again poured out (Rev 19:10; 22:17) Second coming in view Rise of Israel	
	Mystery revealed (Eph 3) ody called out (Eph 2:11-18) es brought in (Rom 11:16-25)		e Mystery ended with the rapture (2Thes 2:7) e Body caught up (2Thess 4:15) entiles cut off (Rom 11:26)	

93

Appendix 2 -- The New Testament Scripture -- Rightly Divided

The New Testament scriptures start with the account of our Lord's earthly ministry in the four Gospels of Matthew, Mark, Luke and John. Following that is the Book of Acts. Then we have what is called the Pauline Epistles (Romans through Philemon). Finally we have the Hebrew church Epistles of Hebrews through the Revelation. That is how we find them laid out in our New Testament. That is actually how the themes of the books unfold in time. The earthly ministry of our Lord Jesus Christ is presented first regarding His ministry to the twelve apostles of Israel. The book of Acts continues with the ministry of the twelve to the nation until mid Act when we find a marked change with the saving of Saul of Tarsus and his call to be the apostle of the Gentiles. There the focus in not on Israel but rather it is a broad based outreach to the lost masses of humanity. The New Testament then has the Pauline Epistles containing a markedly different focus. There the focus in not on Israel but rather it is a broad based outreach to the lost masses of humanity. The elect agency that we find in the Pauline Epistles is no longer the nation of Israel but rather the church, which is Christ's Body and the focus is on the dispensation of the grace of God. The apostle Paul calls the message in these epistles " the preaching of Jesus Christ according to the revelation of the mystery." The Book of Romans presents the foundational doctrine for the mystery while the Book of 2Thessalonians presents the conclusion of it with the catching away of the Body of Christ to its eternal home in heaven. The Book of Hebrews then presents the foundational information to Israel that will equip the nation with the doctrine on how the cross pertains to their program of redemption as God picks up His dealings with them again. Hebrews through the Revelation then takes Israel through the Tribulation Period that follows the Dispensation of Grace and into the promised Kingdom of Heaven.

Half of the New Testament scriptures are about Israel and God's plan for that nation while the other half is about the Church, which is Christ's Body – essentially a Gentile church. The body of doctrine that pertains to Israel is called Prophecy. It is called prophecy because it is what " …God hath spoken by the mouth of all His Holy Prophets since the world began" (Acts 3:21). The other half of the New Testament scriptures (the portion written by Paul, the apostle of the Gentiles) is called the Mystery because it is the body of doctrine that our Lord kept secret until He revealed it to us through Paul for us who live in this present Dispensation of Grace. Paul refers to it as " …The mystery which from the beginning of the world hath been hid in God who created all things by Jesus Christ" (Eph. 3:9). When Paul, the apostle of the Gentiles ,tells us to study to show ourselves approved unto God and be workmen who need not to be ashamed, he is talking about rightly dividing the word of truth – Making the distinction between Prophecy and the Mystery.

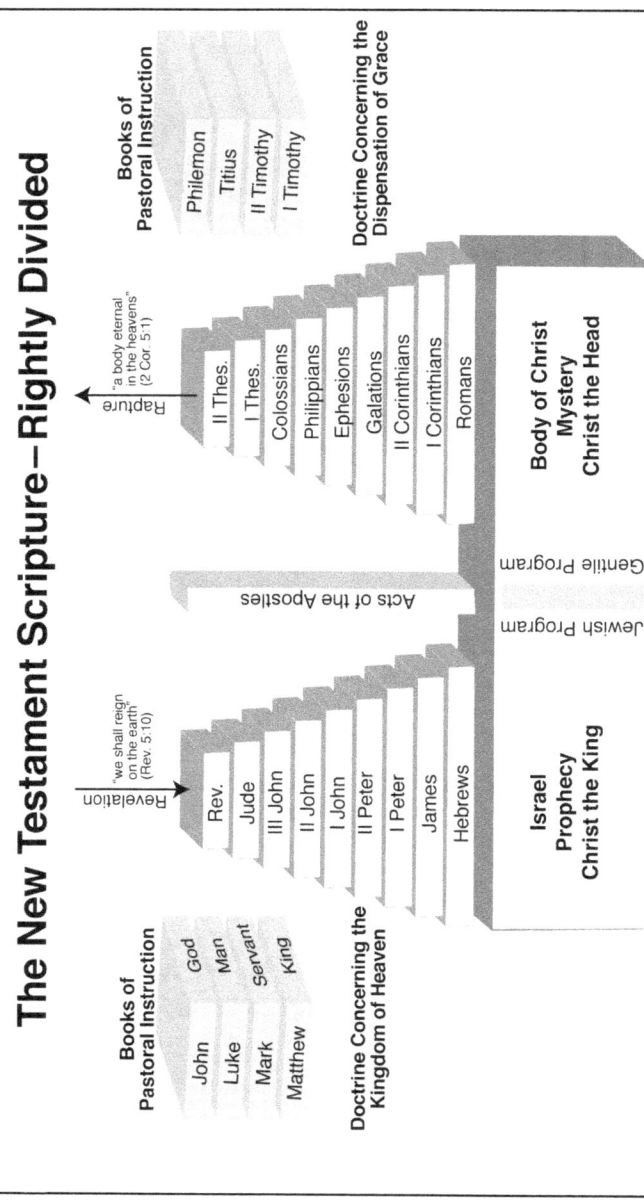

The New Testament Scripture–Rightly Divided

Books of Pastoral Instruction
Philemon
Titius
II Timothy
I Timothy

Doctrine Concerning the Dispensation of Grace

Rapture
"a body eternal in the heavens" (2 Cor. 5:1)

II Thes.
I Thes.
Colossians
Philippians
Ephesians
Galations
II Corinthians
I Corinthians
Romans

Body of Christ Mystery Christ the Head

Gentile Program

Acts of the Apostles

Jewish Program

Revelation
"we shall reign on the earth" (Rev. 5:10)

Rev.
Jude
III John
II John
I John
II Peter
I Peter
James
Hebrews

Israel Prophecy Christ the King

Books of Pastoral Instruction
John
Luke
Mark
Matthew
God
Man
Servant
King

Doctrine Concerning the Kingdom of Heaven

The central person in the Bible is our Lord Jesus Christ. He is the creator of all things in heaven and in earth (Col. 1:16). He is also the one who will reconcile everything in heaven and in earth back to Himself (Col. 1:20). There are two programs by which He will do that. Prophecy is the program by which He reconciles the earth to Himself. The Mystery deals with His reign in the heavens. Point by point the two program are different. The table on the facing page points out those differences. When we note the significance of the differences, we begin to understand how important rightly dividing the Word of Turth is to understanding the Bible

94

Table 3	Prophecy	Mystery
Purpose	That Christ reign on earth (Zech. 9:9-11)	That Christ preeminent in all things (Col. 1:18)
Goal	A Kingdom on Earth (Jer. 23:5)	A Body reigning in heaven (2Cor. 5:1; 2Tim. 2:10-12; Eph. 1:23)
Elect Agency	Redeemed Israel (Ex. 19:5 & 6; 1Pet. 2:9)	The Body of Christ (Col. 1:18, 24)
Relationship to Christ	Christ the King (Isa. 9: 6 & 7)	Christ its the Head of the Body (Eph. 1:21-23; 5:23)
Blessings to the Gentiles	Through Israel's rise (Gen. 22:18; 26:3 &4)	Through Israel's fall (Acts 28: 27-28; Rom. 11:11-15)
Relationship of Jew and Gentile	Israel Supreme (Isa. 60:1 – 3)	Jew and Gentile on the same level (Rom. 3:9; 10:12; cf. 11:30-32; Eph. 2:16-17)
View of Nations	Mainly concerns nation (Isa. 2:4. Ezek. 37:21 – 22)	Concerned with individuals (Rom. 10:12 – 13; 2Cor. 5:14 – 17)
The nature of Blessings to Men	Blessings both Physical and Spiritual on earth (Isa. 2:3; 11:1-9)	All Spiritual Blessings in Heavenly Places in Christ (Eph. 1:3-13; Col. 3:1-3)
View of the Lord's presence on earth	Concern's Christ's presence on earth (Isa. 59:20; Zech. 14:4)	Explains His present absence from the earth (Eph. 1:18-23)
Means of Salvation	Faith demonstrated by works (James 2:14-22)	Through Faith alone (Rom. 3:21 – 26; 4:4 & 5; Eph. 2: 8 & 9)
Relation to the Law of Moses	The Law remains in effect (Mat. 28:20 cf. 23:2; Acts 21:20)	The Law taken out of the way (Eph. 2:14-16; Col. 2:14)
Structure	Concerns God's Nation in the earth (Dan. 2:44; Mat. 6:10)	Concerns a body – a living organism (1Cor. 12:12 & 13; Eph. 4:12 – 16)
Miraculous signs and wonders	Required as evidence of faith (Mark 16:16)	Replaced with unfeigned love (1Cor. 13:8)
Apostleship	Twelve apostles, 12 thrones, 12 tribes (Mat. 19:28)	One apostle to one body (Rom. 11:13; Gal. 2: 8 & 9; Eph. 3:1-13)
Commission	Preach and baptize (Mat. 28:19; Mark 16:16)	Preach without Water baptism (1Cor. 1:17; 2Cor. 5:19 – 21; 1Cor. 12:13 cf. Eph. 4:5)
View of the Lord's Return	His return to the earth to Reign (Acts 1:11 cf. 2:36)	Return to the air to catch the Body of Christ away (1Thess. 4:17)